# Visiting Mom
*An Unexpected Gift*

# Visiting Mom

## AN UNEXPECTED GIFT

*A guide for visiting elders with Alzheimer's*

Second Edition

**ELDER PRESS**
*Sedona, Arizona*

ELDER PRESS, Inc.
2370 W. Highway 89A; Suite 11–#175
Sedona, Arizona 86336-5349
http://www.eldervisit.org

Attention Organizations: Elder Press books and materials are available at
quantity discounts with bulk purchase for educational, training or
business use.  For information or to place an order, please write to:
SPECIAL ORDER DEPARTMENT: ELDER Press; 2370 W. Hwy. 89A;
Suite 11–#175; Sedona, Arizona 86336–5349 or e-mail your request to:
**info@eldervisit.org**

Manufactured in the United States of America by Sheridan Books.

Cover Collage by Jeannie Leighton, Penquillity Designs
Cover Design by Anugito ten Voorde, Artline Graphics

**Library of Congress Card Number: 99-91933** Bell, Sherry M.

Visiting Mom: An Unexpected Gift.  A healing narrative for caregivers,
family and friends who visit elders in nursing homes, assisted living
apartments, hospitals or in the elder's own home.

**ISBN   0-9677081-0-9**

1. Aging–Care–United States.  2. Alzheimer's–United States–Psychology.
3. Caregivers–United States–Attitudes.  4. Alzheimer's–Parkinson's
5. Nursing Homes–United States.

*Note: This book is an adjunct to, not a substitute for, conventional medical
therapy and/or professional legal advice.  For major decisions affecting health or
legal issues, please consult your healthcare professional, physician or attorney.*

*This book is dedicated to*
*Grace Marie Cummings Thomas,*
*a beautiful, loving human being and*
*fortunately for me, my mother.*
*And to all mothers and their children—*
*may we all grow old gracefully.*

## Many Thanks . . .

My mother and I are fortunate to have so many people touch us with love and help as we share this journey. We are very grateful for all the company along the way because this is a victory march and it's not over. Thanking each of you for your companionship is important and we hope to show some of our gratitude in this book. We especially want to acknowledge and thank:

*Our elders*—women and men who live, love and maintain their dignity. Thank you for sharing your journey with us and by example, showing us the kind of wisdom and courage we need in the coming years. *My sister, Kay* and all my other "little sisters" for your enduring love and support.

*Mary Sojourner,* author, editor and National Public Radio (NPR) commentator, for your support and leadership of the "Hardcore Writer's Circle." Thanks also to the merry band of aspiring writers in her 1999-2000 Circles who worked diligently along with me and helped me to *get my words out. My brother Bill, dear relatives, and friends* who continue to share our lives with visits, phone calls and loving greeting cards, all reminders that we are not alone.

*The National Alzheimer's Association* for continuing support of medical research efforts and for the *Arizona Chapter* who develops and maintains critical caregiver services and support groups.

# TABLE OF CONTENTS

*About this book . . .*

### Chapter 1: Change Hurts

Starts at the beginning of the latest leg in my lifetime journey with my mother. The painful changes in our lives due to Alzheimer's disease began about ten years ago.

### Chapter 2: Going Home, Again

Describes the events that started last year. Despite all efforts to avoid this moment, I was forced to move Mom out of our home and into a nursing home–something I never, ever considered doing. I tell about many of the stressful challenges we encountered along the way, as well as the surprising and wonderful lighter times.

### Chapter 3: The Gift

Relates to the remarkable change in my attitude about what we were experiencing. I tell of the eye-opening lessons I learned from Mom, other caregivers and other nursing home residents with Alzheimer's disease.

### Chapter 4: Shocking Secrets

Reveals the ultimate secret ingredient of a "good visit" and discusses seven barriers to address *before* you visit. I call the barriers: resistance, living in the past, change, shock and surprise, frozen feelings, know-it-all, and shadow boxing.

## Chapter 5: Eight Great Habits

Provides a lasting framework for almost any visit. Here I focus on eight great habits to practice every time you visit an elder: preparation, information gathering; a warm greeting; personal attention; clear communication; arts and crafts; physical activity, and a reassuring parting.

## Chapter 6: Five Arts and Crafts

Shows examples of engaging activities that are fun and easy to do during your visit. Creative activities, using basic senses are designed specifically for women elders with progressive conditions.

## Chapter 7: Ten Visiting Guides

Suggests that one kind of visit will not fit every elder or visiting situation. The three building blocks–overcoming visiting barriers; using the eight visiting habits and engaging in fun activities–are combined into ten specific and unique model visits. Each type of visit focuses on meeting the elder's needs as well as the visitor's. Learn how to have the best visit possible whether it lasts for three hours or forty minutes.

I am grateful there is so much I can do when I visit.

# Visiting Mom

# Introduction

Caring for someone with Alzheimer's disease makes for a life filled with every emotion, loaded with contradictions and sprinkled with all kinds of surprises. It's also a time to revisit whatever we think we *know* about life and start at the beginning–it's another opportunity to change and grow. At least, that's how I see things now.

I did not always feel this way which is why I wrote this book in the first place. It is a product of my intense search for better ways to visit with my Mom in the Alzheimer's wing of a nearby nursing home. I began visiting her every other day–to make sure she was getting along all right. I missed her very much and was concerned to know how she was doing on her own, in a place where I could not watch out for her and protect her. It took a while for me to understand that these visits were a blessing and had a second purpose–to help me grow.

It never occurred to me that I would have any problems when I visited with Mom. After all, what could possibly be difficult about a simple visit? You just go there and do visiting-type things, right? Or so I thought. However, only two weeks after moving Mom, I found that I was a stranger in a foreign land–I could not speak the language or find an interpreter. I mindlessly asked Mom a string of questions that fluctuated wildly from sensitive Oprah-like inquiries to harsh police interrogation tactics. As I involuntarily blurted out each question, I could see Mom's growing distress when she couldn't answer. Her responses however, were consistent, "No, I don't think I remember that." This was not quality time for either of us.

I realized that I needed to drastically improve my visiting skills, especially since I did not seem to have any that were suitable for this situation. I gave myself two choices: either sign myself in as her roommate or discover better ways to make our visiting time caring and interesting.

*Visiting Mom* is a healing narrative filled with encouragement and insight for all men and women caring for and caring about elders, especially elders with Alzheimer's disease or with a similar progressive condition. The strength of this book is its focus on visiting our mothers—birth mothers, grandmothers, adopted mothers, step-mothers, and mothers-in-law.

In these pages we take a fresh look at the role of the visitor and learn more about what we *can do* when our elder is in a nursing home, assisted living apartment, hospital room, hospice bed or in their own home. This book emphasizes understanding and the application of constructive actions—things we can do to help our elders and ourselves through what is surely one of life's most challenging times. *Visiting Mom* is based on research, personal experience and my belief that. . .

*The visit is a gift.*

*Chapter 1:*

# Change Hurts

Grace, my Mom, has always had an even, sweet disposition even though she was fiercely independent, principled and loving. She was born in Friars Point, a tiny town in Mississippi, but when Grace was six years old, her mother decided to seek a new life in a large, metropolitan city. They moved to Detroit, Michigan. Grace did well in school and after graduating from high school, she attended Wayne State University–there she met her future husband.

She spent 22 years as a creative, caring homemaker, wife and mother of three. When Grace was 40, she took what was then a dramatic step and divorced her faithless husband. She immediately took her first full-time job outside the home and returned to college to complete the last three years of a degree in education. I moved to my own apartment while Mom continued to raise my brainy brother and lively teen-aged sister. After we left the nest, Mom lived on her own in a series of warm and attractive apartments. Years later, after a grueling 18-year career as the second woman in the history of the city to hold the position of residential property appraiser, Grace decided to enjoy early retirement at age 62. My brother, sister and I were so very proud of her and all she accomplished that we treated her to a big catered party and her dream trip to Paris.

Shortly after she turned 67, I suggested that she and I find a place large enough for both of us. I saw this new living arrangement as a preventive measure, just in case Mom ever needed looking after in some very distant future. Did I know something even then?

### *The first sign . . .*

We moved in together ten years ago, but within two years I noticed that Mom was becoming quite forgetful. Suddenly it seemed, she had trouble understanding how to work common household appliances—like the toaster. I guess the biggest clue that something was not quite right came when I discovered she could not cook any of the wonderful meals that she was known to create. In fact, she could not remember the most basic steps required to prepare herself a bowl of cold cereal. Several times I found uneaten bowls of cereal hidden in the back of one of the kitchen cabinets. I slowly began to understand that a problem of some sort existed. That's when I started to fix her breakfast cereal, a sandwich, fresh fruit and snacks for lunch before I left the house.

Many more signs of something not quite right forced their way into our lives before I ever considered the possibility that her behavior was more than just natural aging. Living together and caring for her these past years has been and continues to be an honor and privilege, even though my life and activities have been changed by the increasing amount of time necessary to be with her and care for her physically and emotionally. Despite many warning signs . . .

*I never imagined Mom would require*
*more care than I could give her.*

Once I was on a three-day business trip and of course I called Mom to see how she was doing. On this trip I first understood that I could not leave her alone for even one day. I spoke to her about 10 p.m. the first night of my trip. All she wanted to talk about was the *gang of young boys* who were walking around the outside of the house looking for ways to break in. Her voice told me she was terrified. I had not known her to be frightened like this before and I did my best to assure her that she was safe. I doubted that gangs were lurking around our home because we lived in a gated community with 24-hour security guards. However, I cut short my trip and returned home early the next day.

After this incident, my brother Bill relieved me from time to time by staying with Mom when I had to make brief out-of-town business trips or so I could take a few days vacation. My sister Kay took time off from her high-pressure corporate job in Los Angeles to stay with Mom whenever I had to leave for five to seven days at a time.

During these early years, Mom's most dramatic behavior change was "hallucinations". This word really does not begin to describe the surreal, multi-sensory experience that occurs for many elders diagnosed with Alzheimer's or dementia. Grace had almost daily, frightening visitations from various gangs who came into her room each night or stood around suspiciously outside our home. They hassled her and she complained that, "They steal everything I own!" She described them to me many, many times and in great detail–their clothes, voices, the way they looked, their ages, and sometimes their thoughts.

First, there was the group of four or five good-looking *Teenaged Boys*. They were interesting, fun-loving and mischievous but always looking for ways to break into our house. Next came the five or six *Young Girls*. These vixens were sexy and attractive and their only reason for living was to wear tight clothes and flirt. Finally, there was the worst gang–*The Old Men*. These old codgers were suspicious men because they only pretended to be decent. What they really wanted, according to Mom, was a *date!* All three gangs, collectively named, *The People*, stole all of her clothes every day–for years!

*The People* never seemed to actually *do* anything bad to her, but they made her *feel* personally threatened, anxious and fearful. Mom got very angry with me whenever she felt I did not *believe* her. But I was at a loss about how to respond to her complaints since I could not *see* what she saw. However, Mom described the gang members so well and so often that I began to believe I would recognize them the next time they stopped by. I no longer think hallucinations are "all in the mind"–I think they are real to the people who can see them.

I learned to accept Mom's unusual experiences and sometimes joined her in these ethereal sightings. I made up humorous short stories about each gang and what they did with the items they stole from her. Our favorite stories were about *The Old Men.*

Once, when Mom told me that *The Old Men* (all lechers) had stolen every one of her panties, I said they did this so that they could give them to *The Young Girls.* I told her the old men hoped that maybe *The Young Girls* would stop liking *The Teenaged Boys* and start dating them. This scenario always gave her something to think about and we would end up laughing because *The Old Men* were so silly. I wanted to make *The Old Men* funny or too stupid to frighten Mom–or me.

### I'm Not Crazy

*From time to time Grace tells me this as she looks straight in my eyes to make sure I get her point. I know that she is expressing her greatest fear–that not being able to remember things means she is nuts, or even worse that I have recognized her craziness too!*

*I respond directly to her by saying, "No, I don't think you're crazy." Then she demands, "Well, what do you think?" and I say, "I just think you forget sometimes, like everybody else." She usually has to think about this for a second, then she seems calmer, less agitated.*

Of course Mom hid everything she treasured (glasses, panties, teeth, etc.) from these gangs every day. Once, after days of searching all three floors of our home we could not find her beloved purse. At Mom's unrelenting insistence, we went to the police station and filed a report. While the kindly officers took Mom's statement, they discreetly stole glances at me.

She calmed down for a few days afterward because I reminded her that the police said they would "start a search to find her purse." This was very important because having her purse with her at all times (even under her pillow with one hand clutching the strap as she slept) was a primary concern for several years. Only recently have I begun to understand just how important this police report was to her and how devastated she must have felt when she thought she lost her most prized possession. I believe that her purse represented her identity (driver's license, Social Security card, library card, etc.), her financial stability (cash and checkbook), her history and especially her greatest treasure–her memory.

In one of my many efforts to keep *The People* from getting into our house, I had a very expensive security door and whole-house burglar alarm system installed. However, Mom's purse, glasses, panties and everything else she valued was hidden and re-hidden daily. When she could not find whatever she was looking for, she spent hours and hours searching her room, furiously slamming doors and banging dresser drawers. I sometimes helped her look for the missing items in hopes of calming her down. After one of these particularly frustrating searches, I began to give serious thought to asking the police to put out an APB (All Points Bulletin) to arrest all of *The People*.

The day came, however, when I knew I was in over my head. According to Mom, *The Old Men* had gotten into her room the night before (they now came through the *walls* since they couldn't get past the new security door), stood silently in her room and without her knowing it . . .

## The Old Men Strike Again!

*"They stole my teeth!" Mom cried. I knew we had to find them. We turned the house upside down for twelve straight hours. That's twelve hours of a non-stop monologue about The Old Men and, "How terrible they are to steal a person's teeth!" Near the end of this mind numbing search, I remembered to create a new story.*

*I told her, "None of The Old Men had any teeth and they only borrowed your teeth because they were hungry. They needed them to eat. They went to McDonald's for a big hamburger and fries and they will bring back your teeth as soon as they are finished eating." Two days later we finally found the darn teeth. They were stuffed into a pair of socks at the back of the linen closet. (I'll bet The Old Men couldn't find them either!)*

About this time, I started attending meetings of the Alzheimer's Support Group in Southfield, Michigan. I did not go because I thought Mom had Alzheimer's disease; I had no idea what that was. Also, Mom was very healthy and we had never known her to be sick. I went because I felt that since this group focused on aging, they could help me understand and deal with Mom. I was fortunate to find a group with a sensitive, knowledgeable leader and brave family members who freely shared their experiences. They helped me begin to understand some of the profound changes in Mom's behavior. Finally, they gently led me to the painful and inescapable conclusion: Mom had many typical behaviors and symptoms of Alzheimer's disease. Months later. . .

*Two doctors delivered the official diagnosis.*

Mom and I had been living together for eight years when after much discussion with my brother and sister I decided to retire early from corporate life and move to Arizona. We spent a long time considering Mom's ability to move and adjust to a new setting. I started talking with her about a year before we actually moved to help prepare her for our new home. We briefly discussed moving nearly every day. When I asked how she felt about moving, Mom's answer was always the same: "I'm sure it will be O.K., as long as we're living together."

By this time I understood that Mom's health situation would not get better, and at the same time I unrealistically thought she would not get worse. I desperately wanted things to stay the same, for time to stand still so that we could continue our lives together. Despite the increasing hours of care she needed, I stubbornly refused to acknowledge what was actually happening to her. In reality, I was too anxious and exhausted to let myself know the truth. Denial was now my first name.

Our move, some 2,400 miles from Michigan, went remarkably well. Mom surprised me by easily accepting our new and dramatically different home environment. However, I could see that her battle with Alzheimer's marched right along. Even though I now knew Mom had Alzheimer's, I was still surprised to find that she didn't remember the Michigan home where we had lived for the past eight years. She could not seem to comprehend that we lived in a different state or that we lived in a new home. My greatest problem after we moved to Arizona was that Mom would come to my room several times each night to awaken me. I was usually jolted awake only to find her face mere inches from mine or to hear her loudly calling me from the foot of my bed. Most of the time she wanted assurance and protection from *The People*.

I was amazed to learn that *The People* had followed her all the way across the country! But this discovery was nothing compared to my total astonishment when I talked with other caregivers in Arizona who had also moved from "back east". They said their elders were also visited by some of the same roving gangs–especially the *Young Boys!* I began to worry that Mom would want to call in the FBI now that *The People* had crossed interstate lines.

Grace rarely took naps during the day. How she managed to go on day after day with so little sleep is difficult to imagine. It was some time before I realized that in the previous seven years, I had not had more than two hours of unbroken sleep at a time. When Mom was not directly waking me, I lay half-asleep, listening as she slammed drawers and cabinets from one end of the house to the other. I had to know what she was doing. I can't nap during the day either–Mom always told us that only lazy people sleep in the day time!

About seven months after moving to Arizona, Ida, our new next-door neighbor, gently but firmly insisted I go to the local Alzheimer's support group with her. Her husband had Alzheimer's also. She saw that I was exhausted and incoherent from continued lack of sleep. This group was similar to my Michigan group, but the Arizona members seemed to be even more open to communicating with each other, both during and between the meetings.

I sure needed this level of support when I was awakened at seven o'clock one morning by loud knocking on our front door. I still felt groggy but I was instantly wide awake when I opened the door to find a uniformed police officer on my porch. I looked over at the police car in our driveway and saw that Mom was in the police car!!

The lady officer told me Mom had been wandering around the neighborhood knocking on people's windows. As I looked over at Mom in bewilderment, she cheerfully called out to the policewoman, "That's my daughter!" I helped Mom out of the car and thanked the officer for returning her. She said her mother has "the same problem". I was terrified because I had no idea that Grace was gone. How long had she been out there? This was very serious. I had failed again.

When I shared this experience with my support group, several people talked about their positive experiences with the nearby *Eden Day Care Center*. They said a driver would pick-up and deliver Mom back home. This meant I would have free time from 8:30 a.m. until 4:00 p.m. three days a week. Mom is very private and quite shy so going to the Center would be an entirely different experience for her. I worried about how she would accept it. I feared that she would not like the group activities. Fortunately, I was dead wrong on both counts.

The Center is very well-run with a high staff-to-client ratio. They excel in providing interesting activities for people with dementia and Alzheimer's disease. I learned that Mom was "ready to go home" each day right after lunch for the first month, but she still seemed to enjoy her time there. I felt her experience was positive because she was never reluctant to go when the white bus came to pick her up in the mornings. Occasionally, when she returned from the Center I asked her, "How did your day go?" She always answered, "The people are very nice," and "I don't remember anything bad. . . so it must be all right!"

I began to think I could live my life during the three days each week Mom was at the Center until I had a frightening false alarm. I was brought sharply back down to earth the day the "pink cat" came into our lives. For the first time ever, I had thoughts of moving Mom to a more secure environment–a nursing home.

### The Pink Cat
*One morning I awoke about 5:30 a.m. to find myself nose-to-nose with KoKo, my sleek white cat. Her head was resting innocently on the next pillow. I immediately closed my eyes again because I thought I was dreaming. However, when I opened my eyes, I confirmed what I thought I saw before. KoKo was a bright pink color! I was instantly and fully awake.*

*KoKo did not seem to be in any pain and joyfully allowed me to examine her all over. Her underside was still white and half of her face remained white, but the rest of her body was the color of Pepto-Bismol! When Mom's cat, Patti saw KoKo, she hissed and socked her in the nose. KoKo seemed to know she was being treated differently because of her "color" and she started acting uncharacter-istically subdued. Our cats have never been outside so I searched all through the house for evidence of something pink she could have gotten into. I found nothing.*

*I got Mom up early and fixed her breakfast so I could look through her room. Nothing pink. After Mom left to go to the Center, I sat with my head in my hands. I just knew Mom had done something terrible to the cat. I resigned myself to thinking that the time had come to move Mom to a safer environment.*

*My despair was suddenly interrupted as I noticed
movement outside on our patio. I was amazed to see
KoKo, my pink cat, walking slowly toward the doors to
get back inside the house. How could she have gotten
out? Since she was walking from the direction of Grace's
room, I ran back there and found Mom's window slightly
open–without a screen. In a flash of belated insight, I
knew what had happened. For whatever reason, Grace
removed her screen and hid it under her bed. KoKo
sensed her opportunity to get outdoors. She had jumped
out the window, rolled in Arizona's trademark red dirt,
climbed back through the window and crawled into my
bed to rest from her deliciously forbidden adventures.*

The pink cat mystery was solved and Mom didn't have to move, however, I realized that my thinking had been muddled, very muddled, when I thought Mom had been cruel to KoKo. I had been listening to several media psychologists analyze reasons behind the Columbine high school massacre. They determined that a common thread among the killers was their cruelty to animals! For just a few uncomfortable moments, I began to wonder if Mom had fallen into this category. I was not thinking clearly at all.

Mom and I resumed our daily routines. But nothing stays the same. On another one of the days Mom was home with me, I saw her walking outside in our back yard and she was dressed in only a blouse, shoes and of course, she had her purse! I calmly got her back inside.

I remembered not to chastise her, but I did ask, "Mom, why were you walking around outside with no clothes on?" She looked down at her bare legs and replied in a slightly irritated voice, "Oh, that's nothing." She held out the bottom of her blouse to prove that she was wearing clothes. I asked again, "What were you doing out there?" "I was looking for the bathroom," she snapped back at me as if any fool would know that. How long had she been out there?

Once again, I had no idea she was gone. I thought I had been even more conscientious about keeping an eye on her since the police brought her home months earlier, but now things were falling apart–again. As I began to review everything I was doing to keep Mom safe, fed, clean and occupied, I made an unnerving discovery about my own daily activities. I determined that for the past several years, I was only able to focus on anything–cooking, reading, bathing, or talking on the phone–for 15 minutes at a time.

Except for the time Mom was at the Center, she was almost always in the same room with me. This had been our pattern for the past eight years. I was finally realizing the tremendous physical cost of maintaining full awareness of where Mom was and being involved in what she was doing 24 hours a day, seven days a week–every week.

I continued to have trouble sleeping even though I had recently discovered the benefits of giving Mom time-released Melatonin (a natural herb) that really helped her rest for most of the night. Now she was waking me up only two or three times each night instead of the usual ten to twelve times. I didn't think I could take anything to relax me or help me sleep because I couldn't risk finding that Mom had left the house again.

I can talk about what my life was like during this period, but I can only imagine what Mom was experiencing. When I imagined her view, based on what I knew about this disease, from our time together, from what she said and her actions, I was stunned...

## In Graceland
*5:45 a.m.*
*Where am I?*
*Oh. This is my place. Where is everything? Oh, hi Patti-girl. Did you have a good sleep last night? (Mom reaches down to pet her yawning cat.) Are you hungry? (Me-ow!) O.K., let's go get you something to eat.*

*I wonder where the food is. Uh, oh, I've got to pee. Where's the bathroom? Oh no, I don't see it. Hmm, here's a nice thick rug. I'll go here. There. Good, you can't see a thing. O.K., now, where's the paper? The People probably stole it. They steal everything I own! Oh well, this blue rag (a silk blouse) will do. There.*

*Where's my clean panties? They're not in this drawer. (slam) Oh yeah, I hid them real good from The People. (slam) I hope they didn't find them. This is bad, now I can't find them either. They're not in this drawer (bang, slam). Where are they? I've never seen anything like this! Why do they pick on me? (slam, slam) I've never done anything to them, but they steal all my things. I don't know why, I don't bother anybody. (crash) I would never take their things. (slam, bang, slam)*

*I'm going to tell Sherry that we have to move away from this place—it's the worst place I have ever lived in in my life! . . . Oh, look, my favorite shoes. Thank God I found them! But these aren't the right shoes. Where are my good shoes? Brrrrr, it's cold in here, where's the hot? (Meew, meew, meew.) O.K., O.K. Let's go, Patti. Let's go get your food. Here's a nice dress, I'll put it on. At least The People left me something to wear. Oh good, my slippers. Mmm, they feel good. O.K., let's go Patti. (Mee-yow!) Let's walk this way. Is the food in here? Hmmm, nice pretty blue towels in there. No food here. Let's keep going. Where did this room come from? I never saw it before in my life! What's going on, where are we? Come on Patti, let's go . . .What's this place? Must be a laundrymat. Those are some big white things. (MEE Oow!)*

*O.K., I'm trying to . . .oh, heeere's the place. This is where the good stuff is! (Meooow, mew.) O.K. (slam) I'm looking, (slam, bang) I can't find the food in here. (bang, rattle) Do you know where it is? (bang) (MEEOW!) I don't see anything! (slam, slam)*

*Here Patti, you can have some of my breakfast. Sherry left it on the table for me. Want some good Raisin Bran? (Meow, mew.) I'll put it in your bowl. (M-E-OW!) What's the matter? Why are you backing away? It's fresh! (M-e-Y-O-O-w!) You don't like it? Look Patti, see, I'm eating it, it's good. Wait, I'll put some yummy banana slices on it. Umm, yum. (MRRL\*&#!!) O.K. See if I care. . .Oh well. Let's see if we can find Sherry. I wonder if she's awake? Come on good girl. . .now which way should we go? (Meow?)* 6:30 a.m.

29

## *Making THE decision*

Once I realized that Grace was in real danger of wandering away from home and possibly hurting herself, I had to admit that I could not do enough to keep her safe. I could not control the situation anymore. Had I ever? Oh, no. No. No. No.

I half-heartedly began exploring places to move Mom. I checked out every place within a reasonable driving distance and finally settled on a well-publicized and modern facility about 20 minutes away. Mom and I went there together three times and twice she was interviewed by the administrator. I went there two additional times on my own. I thoroughly discussed Mom's abilities and described ways that Alzheimer's has affected her behavior. The administrator consoled me by sharing her personal experience with her own mother whom she said has Alzheimer's also. Privately, we specifically discussed Mom's wakefulness at night. I was repeatedly assured that Mom and the other Alzheimer's residents would be looked after at all times like they were "under a microscope."

Later, I met the head nurse who also assured me that she understood Alzheimer's because her own mother had it and lived in another facility. Mom was assigned her own one-bedroom apartment on a newly built wing *"especially for people with dementia and Alzheimer's."*

Once the decision was made, my sister and I spent several thousand dollars to furnish Mom's new apartment. Grace and I also shopped together to pick out things she liked. I could not figure out a good way to talk about the move with Mom. Since we are so close, some of my friends have asked me why I never told her about going to the nursing home. I asked myself this question many times before I began to understand my own reasoning. By the time I actually understood Alzheimer's disease, identified her behaviors and symptoms, and found two doctors to confirm this diagnosis (a period of about two years), Mom's ability to understand and reason had diminished significantly.

The word "Alzheimer's" and the complex and depressing idea of a terminal illness involving damage to the brain were too much for Mom to understand. The memory and reasoning cut-off dates for her had already passed. I also sensed that she just did not want to know. This made my early attempts to discuss a disease of the brain with her frightening and confusing–for both of us.

I think she understood some of what I was saying one day because about an hour after we talked, she casually, but firmly announced, "I will NEVER have an operation!" I never mentioned the word operation, but to her way of thinking if there was something wrong in the brain, an operation was sure to follow. Her own mother died suddenly at age thirty-six following complications from a supposedly routine appendix operation. Grace was only seventeen at the time. She never forgot.

### What, Me Worry?
*One day Mom and I were sitting outside on the patio looking at a calendar. It had the kind of colorful artwork that she likes so much. I told her that the beautiful pictures were made by men and women who had Alzheimer's disease. She frowned for a moment then asked, "What is Alzheimer's?" I explained, "It is a disease that some older people get. It affects their brain and how they think."*

*She just said, "Oh," but she seemed to be thinking about what that would be like. I asked, "Mom, what would you do if you had Alzheimer's?" Grace smiled and replied, "I have enough things to worry about now without thinking about something like that!"*

### I was a mess.

I felt she would strongly protest moving to a "home" it also meant separation from me. I thought I would never be able to explain it to her or get her to go. I imagined all kinds of complete emotional disasters on both sides. In fact, I knew of two caregivers who drove their elder up to the door of the nursing home only to find it impossible to coerce or force them out of the car. Both caregivers had spent considerable time discussing the move and reasons behind the decision before arriving, but it didn't help.

At the heart of my dilemma was the sure knowledge that Mom would pick up on my complete despair, fear and dread. I could not hide any of my feelings whenever I tried to talk about what I was planning. To make matters worse was the fact that I was getting physically weaker every day. Years and years of broken sleep had taken a tremendous toll on my body and mental state. I had been vomiting every night for over a year. I knew that one or both of us had to go somewhere.

I arranged for Mom's new furniture to be moved while she was at the Center for the day. Fortunately for us, my sister came from Los Angeles to help me make the hardest part of the move. Kay did everything possible to help Mom and me get through this ordeal. I would have been in complete disarray without her caring support. I was in a zombie-like state while Kay quietly

led us through the final admission and settling-in process.
I told Mom that she would be staying there so she could be
looked after and I could go back to work. Mom looked bewil-
dered. I saw her expression as we were leaving the building.
I hope never to see the fear and anger that I saw on her face
in this or any other lifetime. I felt like my entire body was
made of hardened cement. I was amazed my knees bent to
walk.

### This remains the single worst day of my life.

Despite all my years of effort to prevent and then delay
moving Mom, it had actually happened. Even writing about
this day now makes me return to the deep grief that is still not
far from the surface. I did not shed a single tear that day. I
was too far past crying. The administrator advised me not to
visit for five to seven days so that Mom could have a chance
to get adjusted. I knew I could physically stay away, but I
could not resist the urge to call the administrator two days
later to inquire about Mom. I was not prepared for what
happened next.

### Her report stopped my breath!

She said Mom had been very disruptive during the nights,
going into other resident's rooms and asking them to help her
look for her mom. She went on to tell me, *"We had no idea
about the extent of her problem. We just aren't set up to handle
people with Alzheimer's!"* Before I could speak, she made
matters worse by advising me to "Talk to her and leave a note
on her door reminding her not to leave her room at night!"
This woman clearly knew nothing about Alzheimer's disease.
She was the same creature who had thoroughly interviewed

Mom and me several times and told of her own mother's Alzheimer's. I couldn't believe my ears! I literally jumped in my car and raced to rescue Mom.

When I arrived my first sight of Grace sent angry shock waves through my body. Mom was highly agitated and talking loudly to the nurse when I arrived. *"I want to get out of this place now!"* She had on shoes, but no socks to keep her feet warm, but it was her hair that frightened me most. It was standing on end, and looked like she had just been electrocuted! What terrible things had happened to her in only two days? I instantly understood homicidal urges. I also realized how important my own actions and demeanor would be to Mom. I re-focused my energy on her well-being and went over to her and held her tightly in my arms. She seemed instantly relieved and gave me a warm smile as soon as she saw me.

We walked slowly up to her room so we could talk and calm down. After a while, I got her to sleep, but only because she was exhausted and shaken. I, however, was wide awake throughout that very long dark night. I used the time to center myself and to plan what I was going to do to the criminals who misrepresented their services and mistreated Mom. Of course I was taking Mom out of there first thing in the morning. I would have to figure out the next steps for us later, after I was sure she was all right, but first, I had one more disturbing experience.

At seven o'clock the next morning, an aide ran breathlessly up to the door and knocked twice. She stuck her head inside the room and called out, "Grace, it's time to get up!" Then she closed the door and raced on to the next room. I sat there stunned. This is what they meant when they assured me that Mom would "have help getting out of bed and dressing every day?"I remembered seeing several other staff racing through the hallways each time I visited before Mom moved in.   Now, I tell everyone:   If you see staff members running up and down hallways like they are being chased by a pack of hungry coyotes, it usually indicates they are seriously understaffed. This might also be an indicator that staff shortages mean the remaining people are working 16-hour shifts.  Now, I know these are dangerous conditions and greatly limit quality care. In this instance, they were sure signs of a substandard facility. I could not get Mom out of that joint fast enough.

Once I got her resettled at our home, I wrote a letter to the facility clearly describing what they promised and what had happened instead.  I made sure they understood that several lawsuits and natural disasters would happen if I did not get all my money back immediately.  I wished that money had been the only thing at stake.  These little pieces of paper were entirely worthless compared to the well-being of my mother. Money meant nothing to me.

So there we were.  After only three days I was again making moving arrangements, but this time I was moving Mom's new furniture into our garage.  Fortunately, Mom seemed to have absolutely no memory of being in *that place*.  How could I ever put her through this again?  What did I do wrong?  My self-confidence was gone, I did not trust myself.  What could I do now?

**We were back to square one.**

*Visiting Mom*

Chapter 2:
# Going Home, Again

Grace resumed attending the Center three days a week, while I struggled to get through each day. Once again, I started to find out about housing/care alternatives–this time with the help of the state social services for the aging. I discovered Mom could move into a special Alzheimer's wing connected with the nursing home that sponsored my support group. This facility was not an option I could afford before, but now, with state assistance, Mom could go there. This place was also recommended by friends of mine and it was on the state's "approved" list. I was still suffering from lack of confidence about knowing what was true and what was not. I thought I would never forgive myself if I made another poor choice and moved her into yet another crummy place. How could I be sure? I wanted guarantees, but I was out there on my own.

I was angry and scared, I was having a major spiritual conflict. I asked God for guidance and wisdom and the best life for Mom. Quietly, I confessed that I did not trust God to take good care of Mom. God had already fallen down on the job since Mom had this disease in the first place. Yes, I was angry, then I realized I was angry at God. I remembered an old play where an actor shook his fist at God! I was horrified that he was so stupid and I thought it only showed how little he knew or loved God. But now I felt just as furious as that man must have felt. How could a loving God do this to a sweet person like Grace? Nothing made sense to me.

I was at a time in my life when I thought I should know something about life; instead, I knew nothing about anything. Not only did I have to figure out everything about Mom and Alzheimer's, but now, in whatever spare time I could find, I had to re-define what I thought and felt about God. I wanted to get this settled quickly because my growing confusion, disappointment and anger were preventing me from helping her.

I did not do this soul-searching willingly. I was driven completely by desperation but I had to reconnect with my spirit. Many days of intense inner turmoil followed but I was determined. Finally, I began to feel that my prayers had been answered because I slowly began to understand that *everything* is part of the Plan. God doesn't make mistakes or forget anyone or give special treatment. Our job is to choose our way and grow through our experiences—the ones we choose and those we want to avoid. I was no longer angry, at anyone. I felt I could move on.

During the next two months I pushed myself to do one or two things each day and somehow managed to plow through another series of lengthy interviews with nursing home staff. I was still numb with grief and this time I arranged to move her by myself. I knew I had to do this for both of us. Once again, I told Grace that I had to go back to work and that she would be staying with these "new people" so she wouldn't be left alone. I reminded her that she stayed there for a few days before (in respite care). Of course she did not remember, but it seemed to be O.K. with her. The administrator here was also the leader of my support group. Pam arranged to come and guide us through the initial hours of adjustment. I hoped it would be easier than before, but I was wrong again. In some ways it was worse.

## The Boss

*Grace and I were rudely greeted by her new roommate the second we entered their room for the first time. The roommate was very irritated. She told us, "No one is to enter my room without asking for and receiving my permission first!"*

*Pam reminded the roommate that they had discussed the fact that she would be sharing the room several days ago and again last night. The roommate declared, "Nobody told me anything, but it does not matter because I am not sharing the room with anyone. I don't have roommates!" Pam gently, but firmly told her again that she would be sharing the room and attempted to introduce Grace to her.*

*The roommate seemed to sense that she had lost this round, but she wanted the last word. She then loudly announced, "If I have to have a roommate, then I want it understood that I am the boss in here and what I say goes. She (nodding toward Grace) will have to do whatever I say and follow my rules!" Well. Mom had been sitting silently throughout this hostile monologue, but this last statement was too much for her. Mom quietly, but very firmly said, "I don't have to take that s..t."*

Pam quickly intervened and again told the roommate that she, like everyone else, would have a roommate. She assured me that the roommate would come around and soon accept Mom. So, with the help of several staff, we began to put Grace's things in the closets and dresser without another word from the roommate. I used all my remaining strength to keep from breaking down and sobbing in front of Mom. I wore my darkest sunglasses so she couldn't see my eyes.

A short time later, Mom and I were slowly walking in the hallway talking about making friends and joining in the activities with the others. Grace turned to me and said, "I think something is wrong with that woman." I told her the roommate was unhappy today and we talked about what she could do to make the situation better, like make friends with some of the other women who seemed to be very nice. She agreed, "That's a good idea." After about an hour, I finally let go of her hand and watched as the aide led Mom away from me and into the dining room.

I just stood there. I could not move. New words would have to be created to describe the profound helplessness or the sharp, burning pain in my throat and stomach. But the most intense pain was in what was left of my heart.

### I thought my heart would burst.

Pam told me I shouldn't see Mom for one or two weeks so that she could get adjusted. Thankfully, some of my friends from the support group who were visiting their husbands, wives or mothers at that facility gave me daily reports for the first few days about how Mom was doing. They looked for her and spoke to her. Each of them told me that she seemed to be doing "very well" and that she was participating in the activities and talking with the other residents. These reports all sounded good, but I wanted to see for myself.

After five days I visited her for the first time. To my great relief, my friends were right! Mom was relaxed and glad to see me, but not desperate. We had a good first visit and she seemed to accept that I had to "go back to work." I assured her that I would be back to see her in "two days." She never once asked to go home. Later I discovered that ...

*Mom did not remember our home.*

*Visiting Mom*

*Chapter 3:*
# The Gift

On the drive down to visit Mom the first few times, my mouth was as dry as sand, my eyes watered and my stomach knotted up. I live in Sedona, Arizona, probably one of the most dramatically beautiful places in the country. However, I suddenly developed a strong dislike for the stupid-looking rocks that made up the formerly beautiful mountains. The cloud formations now looked obscene, the color of the red rocks began to irritate me and the perfectly shaped evergreens with their abundant growth got on my last nerve.

I was flooded with conflicting thoughts and feelings about visiting Mom. I was so caught up in my emotions that the closer I got to the nursing home, the more fear and dread I experienced. I imagined that by the time I got there I would be frozen at the front door and never go inside. I wanted this whole experience just to go away. These early visits were the worst times for several reasons. First, when I reached the nursing home I had to walk down the miles-long hallway to my Mom's section. The sight of the older people lined up parallel to the walls, imprisoned in their wheelchairs was intimidating. The sounds of their words as they called out for assistance or attention was very depressing. I had to get past these wheelchair-bound obstacles each time I went to see Grace. Each visit became harder and harder for me to walk-the-walk. However, what really got to me was the occasional, but startling assault on my olfactory senses–the sharp and curiously offensive smell of someone that had just messed themselves.

*I was terror stricken about "the smell".*

I started sniffing as soon as I opened the front door to the nursing home. I admit that "the smell" was not all over the nursing home and most of the time it wasn't in the air at all, but finding out exactly where it *might* be lurking turned into an obsession. I never knew when I would be ambushed by *it* and overcome with nausea. Each doorway I approached became the potential source of a surprise *smell* attack. I walked quickly, frantically looking to the left and right, trying to see through the walls, to see the source of my fears before my nose found out where *it* was hiding.

I finally arrived, out of breath and wide-eyed at the nurses' station in my Mom's section. This is when I realized I had been holding my breath all the way down the unending hall–just in case. To make matter worse, I began to hate for my visits to end–because that's when the real nightmare began. . .

## The Gauntlet

*Once again I had to walk down the hallway. This time
the residents, armed with their wheelchairs appeared to
be lying in wait–strategically placed in a herringbone-
like attack formation designed to block my escape. As I
zig-zagged between and around the wheelchair barri-
cades, the ladies would actually reach out and touch or
hold on to me while the men looked in my eyes and gave
me tentative smiles.*

*I quickly learned: no smiles, no hellos and absolutely, no
eye contact. But I couldn't close my ears to their words–
"Hi ya, honey, you look nice today, let me tell you
something. What's your name?" and "See you next time,
O.K.?" They sounded so innocent and harmless.*

*Somehow, I also heard the things they did not say out
loud, the silent words that somehow shouted from their
quiet bodies–"I'm lonely, I'm afraid; talk to me. Please
share some of your kindness with me." I can only
imagine the courage it must take for them to put their
deep desire for attention on the line and risk repeated
rejection from visitors like me–time after time.*

*By the time I finally burst through the exit door I was
overwhelmed by the residents' needs and frightened by
the helpless people who asked for so little. I had to lean
over and take several deep breaths before staggering to
my car. Running the gauntlet was one long panic attack.*

Why couldn't I give them my attention? It was over a month
before I could walk the halls peacefully and comfortably greet
the residents.

Mom has been in this new place (I still have great difficulty saying "home") for several months now. Yes, I count the weeks and months and know the exact day and date she moved. She seems to have settled in as well as anyone could ever expect and always seems to be calm and relaxed when I come to visit her. But it was the startling discovery I made only two weeks after my first visit that compelled me to write this book. I did not believe it could be possible, but . . .

*We were running out of things to talk about!*

I was startled to find that as close as Grace and I have always been, I really did not *know* her. I could not imagine how I would ever handle this new and unsettling situation since I was still trying to manage all the physical and emotional changes in both our lives as a result of Alzheimer's disease. However, I remembered that my first priority for now was to my mother and her needs. Some caregivers talk about their experience in placing an elder in a nursing home and how glad they are to "get my life back." I never quite understood what they meant . . .

*I wanted my Mom back.*

After the first two weeks of visiting Mom, I slowly began to awake from my unchecked spiral into visitor's hell. I had to really think about what was important to me and why. Then I had what some residents in Sedona call a "Pink Moment."

### A Pink Moment
*One evening I was looking out my living room window on a panoramic view of sky and mountains just after a light summer rain. The dusty, rose-colored mountains*

*suddenly radiated a golden glow as if several spotlights were focused on them. They revealed horizontal stripes of lavender rock sprinkled with sparkling flecks of gold dust. Then in the sky I saw a fat, brilliant rainbow. It arched so high that it hurt my neck to look up and it was so many miles wide that it seemed to start in one canyon and drop down somewhere behind a distant mountain range. I didn't know that rainbows could touch the ground.*

*Then I discovered a second, even larger rainbow on top of the first–a double rainbow! It was fuzzy looking and not as bright, but more remarkable in its grand size. As I experienced this marvel of nature, I entered into a wondrous place and time. The air was suddenly peaceful, silent, loving and filled with all the wisdom of the universe. . .all around me and inside of me. . . I was part of it. I rested completely. When I returned, I felt energized and grateful. Somehow, at that moment–that "Pink Moment"–I just knew . . .*

### Visiting mom is a beautiful gift.

This was a startling idea for me–the visit as a gift, something I could treasure. I had been so busy with negative, confused thoughts and feelings that I could not see the wonderful opportunity I had in front of me. I could hate Mom's Alzheimer's and be filled with the resentment, grief and destructive anxiety of a helpless victim, or I could accept her situation as an invitation to create a new, loving environment for her.

Ever since Mom was diagnosed with this always fatal disease, I had been living in a dark, hopeless world of grief. It has no definable beginning and there is no light at the end of the tunnel. This is what I brought with me when I visited–this is *not* where I wanted to live. Something had to change. Suddenly, I understood that I did not have to stay there. I felt a jolt of strength throughout my body and I knew I could somehow deal with the advance of her disease and help her at the same time. I saw unlimited opportunities to create a positive world for both of us–starting with my new, grateful attitude. I knew in my heart that . .

*It is impossible to be grateful and unhappy at the same time.*

In Iyanla Vanzant's best selling book, *Faith in the Valley*, she writes: "I am in the healing process. Healing is a great deal more painful than fixing. . . but think of it this way, once there is a healing, the problem goes away for good."

**The problem is not Alzheimers,
but my attitude toward it.**

I decided that my visits would be an opportunity to celebrate Mom's life. I go to see her to make sure she knows she is loved and cared for. So, I asked myself: *"What can I do to make our time together fun and interesting for both of us?"* Before this experience, I knew very little about nursing homes, in fact, I had only visited one once before in my life–it was not a happy occasion . . .

## My First Time

*About 25 years ago, Kay and I went to a nursing home to visit Lil, our 78 year-old step-grandmother who had recently broken her hip. Over the years she made sure my brother, sister and I knew that she only tolerated us because of my grandfather. He died when I was only seventeen. Lil had no children, very few friends and no known relatives. Anyway, we brought her a cake and a bottle of wine as treats–these were things she liked and we thought she probably did not get in a nursing home.*

*Everything about her nursing home was worn and, well–shabby. I couldn't figure out why she was in a place like this–it was a place for poor people, very poor people. We were directed down dimly-lit hallways to a crowded pea-green room. I remember only one very dirty window near the ceiling. The room held eight beds and eight old women all dressed in hospital gowns and slippers. Their beds were separated by flimsy curtains–just like a ward in the old movie **Snake Pit**.*

*Kay and I felt very self-conscious as we entered the room because all talk ceased as every eye turned to inspect us. Hurriedly, we spotted Lil in a bed near the door. We greeted her and gave her our treats. She never said a single word, but just looked at each of us quizzically as we talked to her from either side of her bed.*

*Suddenly we heard someone call our names and saw another woman walking towards us with a cane. It was Lil! We were talking to the wrong woman! We had not seen Lil for over eight years and I guess we forgot how she looked.*

*My sister and I tried to hide our embarrassment as we snatched our treats back from the imposter and went over to greet the real Lil. She was so happy to have visitors that she seemed to forgive us immediately. She was clearly pleased that everyone was watching as she led us to her bed near the back of the dim room.*

*The other women made no secret that they were watching and intently listening to our every word. Lil startled Kay and I by proudly introducing us to several of the ladies as her "grandbabies," an endearment that never slipped past her lips in all the years we had known her. We left in about an hour but we never went back or talked about this depressing experience again.*

This sad memory made me think of ways to make Mom's surroundings more home-like and new ways to make sure she felt she was getting caring attention. Just thinking of Lil's drab pea green hospital curtains makes me sad. I found that Martha Stewart made curtains to match Mom's blue flowered bedspread so we hung them over the washed out ones in Mom's room–what a difference! My sister and I hung them (with permission from the administrator) while Mom ate lunch one day. They transformed Mom's space beautifully leaving the other side free for her roommate to decorate or not. This cost about $30 and Grace was delighted.
What a good start!

*Chapter 4:*
# Shocking Secrets

I am amazed at all the stuff that has come up–ideas, habits, assumptions and beliefs for me to examine and reform to fit where I am now. This is when I came upon the simple, but "shocking secret" about visiting Mom . . .

> ***A good visit begins and ends
> with a good visitor.***

Spending time with an elder who has Alzheimer's disease does not fit into commonly held ideas about visiting because of the unpredictable ways that brain damage affects each person. The most jarring distinction is that we have a heavy and ever-increasing responsibility for the quality of our time together as well as for the number of visits that occur. A good visit depends on overcoming our personal barriers and then learning to be a *good visitor*.

We can't expect mom to hold up her end of a conversation, maintain an interest in what we want to talk about, remember our names, or sometimes even acknowledge our presence in the room. Fortunately, there are at least five things we can do to change and improve our visits:

> **Get to Know Mom**–*her past, present and future medical condition; her personality; history; needs and desires; and family relationships.*

> *Examine the* **Shocking Secrets** *and find ways to overcome any damaging beliefs, thoughts and myths about mom, her health and her new environment.*

> *Remember the* **Eight Great Habits** *framework for a good visit and use it during every visit.*

> *Use* **Arts and Crafts** *during almost any visit and bring joy to mom's day.*

> *Experience the* **Ten Great Visits** *to find the best ones for you and mom.*

This chapter describes seven barriers we may bring along with us when we see mom. I suggest ways to overcome them and improve the quality of our visit.

I knew I could not have the best visit possible unless and until I took time to rid *myself* of the barriers I had, as described in the first part of this book. In the following pages, we examine secret barriers created by many adult children. Each one suggests ways to become a more caring, energizing, and peaceful visitor.

The seven barriers that often stand in our path are:

1) *Resistance* to telling the truth to others and especially to ourselves;

2) *Living in the Past* means letting go of our memories and beginning life in the present moment with mom;

3) *Change,* or not changing what we've always done, thought or said even though everything else is different;

4) *Shock and Surprise* occurs frequently if we haven't taken time to learn what to expect;

5) *Frozen Feelings* are dissolved by asking ourselves and answering "hard" questions;

6) *Know-It-All* attitudes about learning medical facts and sharing feelings and fears with our families;

7) *Shadowboxing* and trying to fight mom's ghost from our past when what we really want is peace. Before we visit our mom's home, we need to get our own house in order.

## The 1st Barrier: **RESISTANCE**

This first barrier is one that most of us try to hide from others as well as ourselves. I never heard anyone suggest *not* to visit. Instead, I hear, "You should go, Just stay a little while, You owe it to her," or worse, "What kind of a son/daughter are you?" If this is the first time you have seen these words in print, then it may also be the first time you considered that you even had a choice. You know how you feel when someone doesn't want to be with you. Your mother may have Alzheimer's, but she knows too.

Visiting your mother or anyone with Alzheimer's or a similar disease is often a heartbreaking experience–even under the best of circumstances. I first thought that the "best" visiting situation happened when there was a strong, loving lifetime relationship; great professional and caring staff; and reasonably good physical health of all concerned. However, I discovered that even when we have a positive situation like this, we then face the pain of losing a person who has supported us and brought us much joy. Surprisingly, when our relationship is filled with toxic experiences and painful memories, visiting can be equally, and sometimes more difficult to face because we tend to feel deprived and resent the fact that we may never have what we desire.

In *Making Peace with Your Parents,* Harold H. Bloomfield, M.D. points out that many of us think that to have mixed emotions about our parents is either selfish or ungrateful. As a result, we may *pretend* to be selfless and saintly in the presence of our aging or dying parent when in fact anger or fear is stirring inside us. Every caregiver/visitor has to resolve past feelings and experiences related to mom, themselves and their lifetime relationship.

There are also caregivers who seem to visit *too often.* Is this possible? It happens more often than I would have imagined. How many visits are too many and who determines the right number? Usually, it is someone else who suggests that you may be visiting too much. They see how exhausted you are from the frequent visits and hear how unrewarding these visits are–for everyone. Many times the reason given for frequent visits is to feed mom, sometimes two or three times a day! Why? Eating is one of the most universal, social activities we can share with another person and food is known to be related to love. We perform a needed service and touch mom in a commonly understood way. However, rarely do I hear that their mom actually desires or needs them to feed her or that the visitor actually *wants* to feed their mother. Unfortunately, this caring act can turn into merely "doing your duty." What good does this duty-bound type of visit do for either of you? I'm not sure, and I wonder if it is the type of visit most of us would choose for ourselves.

There are times when I don't want to visit Mom. There, I've said it. I want to delete those words from the page. I am ashamed that I ever had this thought. Why don't I always leap for joy at the thought of visiting Mom in the nursing home? In my more rational and charitable moments, I see just how unrealistic and ridiculous this demand is for me or anyone. We have to tell the truth to ourselves and determine why we may sometimes, or perhaps always, experience *visiting resistance.*

There are other reasons we may *resist* visiting that have to do with our **lack of knowledge** about the aging process in general and about Alzheimer's or similar diseases, in particular. We may secretly say things like, *"I can't stand to see her getting worse,"* or *"She won't even know if I visit or not."* A second reason for not visiting may have to do with our preoccupation with **reliving past** negative experiences with mom, such as *"Mother never seemed to like me,"* or *"She was mean to me."* It may seem easier to hold on to painful memories of mom as if to hold her hostage until she says or does the right thing or begs our forgiveness. Saying the words, *"I know mom has a fatal disease"* is not enough. We need to bring those words into our heart and let them dissolve past hurts.

Some of us stay away because **mom's not perfect** and hasn't lived up to our own fantastic expectations of mothers. Aren't mothers supposed to act according to our ideas? Not in this world.

### Mom is just another human being.

Bloomfield also tells of a way to accomplish the task of understanding and releasing our unresolved feelings about mom. He suggests that we compose a "letter of regrets" to release old hurts. Writing out our memories to voice feelings and thoughts we have held back moves us to create the caring words we secretly longed to hear from mom. At the heart of a good visit is our truthful, compassionate answer to the question: How can I be of service to my mother without feeling burdened, unappreciated and resentful? You are totally responsible for what you say and do when you truthfully answer this question. Resisting only makes it more difficult to have a good visit.

## *The 2nd Barrier:* **LIVING IN THE PAST**

How many times could I start over?  After all the years I had taken care of Mom, all my energies were focused on her–that was my life.  Now that she is cared for by others, what will my life be like?  I could not just pick up where I left off ten years ago.  I'm not that person, whoever she was.  I've got to find out who I am now, what I like and dislike, what thoughts and ideas attract me?   Now I even have to come up with something else to think about besides Mom.  All these years, no matter what else I was doing, I was constantly thinking about her–what and how she was doing.  I still think about her a lot, but not quite as much and certainly not with the feverish intensity I carried with me 24 hours a day–for years.

Coming up with a "new me" is exciting and sad.  Grace seems to have adjusted faster and easier than I have to the changes in our lives, I told my sister recently.  I was so pleased about this that I began to feel I could relax, maybe even take a short vacation.  Five days after I had this thought I had a major bleeding ulcer attack–I really had relaxed!  Everything I had been holding inside came out in a flood.  I spent several days in bed but even in the midst of my serious health crisis, the driver for my recovery was that I wanted to be around for Mom.

As I thought about taking care of my needs for the first time in who knows how long, I began to see the enormous task that lay ahead.  I went to Flagstaff to see my friend Marilyn, a well-known therapist and healer. I needed help putting feelings into words I was not able to understand or say out loud on my own.

When we talked, Marilyn suggested that I might need a "bridge" from the part of my life that was over (ten years of caring for Mom at home) to get to the new life that lay ahead. I could see ways to wrap up the past, but when I got to the bridge part, my deepest fears exploded. I could not envision a bridge! I only saw a wide, bottomless canyon and a very hazy other side. This dark image terrified me. Reluctantly, I discovered that I thought my life might be over without Mom to care for–I had no plans, no dreams–just nothing now that she was gone from our home. Where had I gone?

## *The 3rd Barrier:* **CHANGE**

For ten years my role as caregiver defined my life. I knew this role inside and out. I thought I knew what was expected of me. Even as Grace changed and the disease progressed, I still felt I knew what to do. It was easy to fool myself into believing that Mom was in a suitable environment and I could just sit back and take a breather. No way! Actually I thought I would get some time just to relax, but I was wrong again.

Caring for and about an elder requires that we accept change as a constant in our lives. For example, there continues to be a need to change roommates, move to a new room on a different side of the hallway, adjust medicines, arrange transportation to dentists and doctors, replace panty pads with adult diapers, observe eating patterns, make sure she gets enough water, learn the names of the ever-changing staff and aides, and so forth. Recently, I had an experience that stretched me to my limit, but it made me see clearly that I was the one who needed to change.

### Grace Under Fire
*I had been visiting Mom for about five months when I picked her up to go shopping and browsing in Flagstaff. We always have a great time looking at the sights and walking around. But soon after we left Flagstaff, Grace said, "I feel funny, maybe you should pull over." She lost her lunch, but seemed to be fine after that. When we arrived back at the home, I suggested she rest for a while until dinner. She agreed without hesitation, but her roommate had other ideas . . .*

*The second we opened the door to their room, the roommate came briskly toward us, stood in the entrance and tried to physically block us from coming in the room. "Who said you could come in? I didn't give you permission to enter MY room. If you want to come in, you have to knock and wait for permission," she shouted. I calmly reminded her that this room belonged to both of them and that my mother was going to lie down in her bed. I helped Mom to her bed and pulled the comforter over her.*

*Grace had not said a word, but she did chime in when I said, "This is her bed." The roommate got louder, "I have never seen her before, but it doesn't matter because this is MY room and I don't have roommates." I turned to talk to Mom, but the roommate kept interrupting. She was now standing across from me on the other side of Mom's bed yelling…"If you want to belong to this family, you will have to do what I say. I didn't say she could get in this bed! From now on, you have to ask my permission!"*

*Then the roommate went entirely too far–she snatched the comforter off Mom!! I jumped up, instantly pumped with adrenaline and ready for action, but I stood completely rigid. My eyes locked on the roommate. No words passed between us, but she quickly dropped the comforter and silently went back to her bed. I covered Mom up without further protest from the roommate.*

I had to make sure I did not do or say something I would regret. I reminded myself that the roommate had Alzheimer's too, even though her behaviors are quite different from Grace's. I didn't want to leave Mom alone with this out-of-control woman, but I had to get help. I told Mom I would be right back and left the room in search of the administrator. When I found her I quickly described what had happened. I told the nurse, "This threatening behavior has continued from the first day my Mom came and I want her moved to a new room. She should not have to argue her way into her room everyday."

With my approval, Mom was moved to a new room with a more agreeable roommate the next day. My role and respon-sibilities toward Mom have changed physically, medically and emotionally. My new job description is *visitor/advocate* and I'm still not sure about all that it means. The transition and ultimate change into my new role has been difficult and I kicked and screamed with every step. I realize that change will occur with or without me–it's up to me to decide how I will interpret life now and act in the future.

I want to be there for my mother which means I have to restart my own life–not where I left it years ago when I first began caring for her, but at some new and unknown place in the present. My new job is to redefine how I can care for Grace in this new setting. What do I need to continue to do, what needs to be done differently, and what should I stop doing? Mom's troubling question, "Where's Sherry?" seems more appropriate now, but I want to know, "*Who* is Sherry?"

## *The 4th Barrier:* **SHOCK AND SURPRISE**

All my thinking and planning amounted to nothing during one recent visit when Grace angrily demanded, *"Just who do you think is the mother here?"* Mom's anger and her question were a wake-up call for me. For some visitors, the call comes when mom gets verbally difficult and/or physically combative with you, residents or other caregivers.

I've heard several people say that elders with Alzheimer's are just like children. I have always been uncomfortable with that analogy because Grace is *not* my child. Sometimes I seem to treat her that way or she may feel I'm treating her like a child. Either way, she is bound not to like it and she lets me know. Grace may not know who I am all the time, but she sure knows which one of us is the mother. Any time I mistakenly put myself in the parent role, she responds with sharp expressions of anger or resentment. For her this type of role reversal seems to mean a loss of control and unnaturally reorders her world. She fights back to regain her status.

Because of the type of brain damage associated with Alzheimer's, parts of the brain that have to do with social interactions may be affected in many different ways. Your mom may suddenly show a side of herself never seen before. She may suddenly reveal startling personal information that she would not normally tell you or anyone, for example: *Your brother isn't really your brother; you are not the oldest; I was forced to give away my first child. Your father and I "fooled around" before we married, guess what we did?"* Or, you may be in for another kind of surprise–mom may get very excited during your visit and mess her pants. This could mean that the rest of your time is spent cleaning her up and getting both of you calmed down. The sights and smells of an "accident" are sharp and unfamiliar, but they ignite our imaginations and fears even more than our memories. Sons understandably have a hard time cleaning up mom after an accident, but nobody gets a free ride. This too is a part of life now.

You might happen to come for your visit at meal time and watch mom eat her spaghetti with her fingers, using her hand to wipe the sauce smeared on her cheeks. She might also chew with her mouth open! And what do you do when shortly after you arrive to visit mom suddenly announces that she wants to go back to the activity room to be with her new friends?

### And then, there's . . .

*The other day Grace and I were having a nice lunch outdoors, chatting cheerfully about nothing in particular when she suddenly asked me, "Where's Sherry?" I responded by calmly asking her, "Do you know my name, Mom?" She looked at me with a mischievous smile before answering, "Don't you know?" I said, "Yes, I know, but I want to know if you know." She thought for a moment and replied, "I know who you are, but I'm not going to tell you. You're Whatcha-ma-call-it!" We burst out laughing and continued eating our French fries. . .I quietly told her, "I'm Sherry." She tilted her head to one side and seemed to consider this for a minute before saying, "Well, you may 'think' you're Sherry and you may 'be' Sherry, but. . .**You're not the right Sherry!**"*

Mom has asked me this question, "Where's Sherry?" many times over the past three years–usually at three in the morning. I have never been able to come up with a response.

Mom's sense of humor is a gift but the reality of her memory loss and the thought that I might be lost from her memory feels like a deep cut from a rusty knife. As bad as these experiences are, they remind me that the worst days of Alzheimer's are yet to come. The day is fast approaching when Mom may not know me at all. I used to feel protected from that fate because I look so much like my mother–I thought that she would always recognize my face, it's so like her own.

Sometimes her words and behaviors shock and surprise me. These wake-up calls can suddenly and dramatically turn our time together into the *visit from hell.* When I find I am frequently shocked and surprised, then I know I need to return my focus to preparing and educating myself. Getting past this barrier takes considerable time and effort to learn more about what to expect so that when we visit so we can just . . .

**Let mom be mom.**

*The 5th Barrier:* **FROZEN FEELINGS**

Our connection with our mother is perhaps the most intense emotional relationship we will have in our lifetime. It has many dimensions and is filled with every emotion imaginable. Sometimes "mom" is actually a mother-in-law, adopted mother, stepmother or grandmother which adds another layer of emotional complexity to our relationship. Guilt, anger, grief and relief are the emotions that baffle me the most as I continue to care for Mom.

**Guilt** is an emotion that has been very difficult for me to recognize. I barely remember feeling "guilty" in my entire life. So I didn't even have a name to describe many of the feelings I experienced about moving Mom into a *home*. I thought I did not have any other choice at the time and I could not find anything wrong with the place where I was moving her. Like Mr. Spock on *Star Trek*, I "thought" that feeling guilty made no sense.

Looking back, I wonder if anyone could escape feeling guilt (responsibility) about making such life-shaping decisions for another person. So often I judged myself a failure when something did not go according to my plans or even when it did, but things didn't work out anyway. I had limited myself to an artificial life in a courtroom drama where I sought justice, but only found the harsh verdicts of *not-so-good* and *very bad*. In my mind, the jury usually came back with a guilty verdict and condemned me with a terrible punishment for almost every one of my decisions about Grace's care.

Then there was *anger*. When I finally acknowledged that I was feeling angry, it was in the midst of my worst turmoil with Mom's advancing condition. How could I be angry at her? I *knew* it wasn't Mom's fault that she got Alzheimer's and now required round-the-clock attention and care, but still I was angry. When I finally sorted myself out, the answer was far worse that I initially suspected. However, I wasn't angry with Mom at all, I was angry at God. This realization presented a much greater problem before I understood I could express my real feelings and fears and God would not send lightning bolts.

Next, I tackled *grief*. I have experienced the death of only a few friends or relatives in my life. I discovered that most of my depression surrounding Mom's care was mislabeled and was actually grief. I was numb with grief and had been in this frozen state for at least two years when I discovered this.

Grieving with diseases like Alzheimer's has a murky beginning and I'm still not sure whether it even has an end. This is one of the reasons grief is so hard to identify, but there is another more tangible reason. I understood grieving to occur when someone or something was "gone" and did not exist anymore. This type of narrow thinking did not allow me to see the huge gray grieving area that I was actually experiencing. Grace was not "gone" as she would be if she were dead, she was here with me as flesh and blood–I could see, touch, hear and talk to her everyday. At the same time, she was losing her ability to recognize me, respond to my touch, understand what she heard or say what she was thinking. No wonder I was confused. But grief doesn't end when you tell it to stop, it has a way of doubling back and kicking you when you least expect it.

For several months after I moved Grace, I had great difficulty doing everyday things like going to the grocery store. I increased the number of meals I ate in restaurants, ordered take-out dinners or just didn't eat. This happened mostly because of the problem I had going to the grocery store. . .

### Snap, Crackle & Pop!

*My problems started as soon as I got to the store and realized that I needed a shopping cart. For the past fifteen years Grace and I have done our grocery shopping together every week. She always took charge of the cart while I loaded it with our groceries. I never pushed the cart before and resented the fact that I had to push the darn thing now. But, then the real trouble started.*

*It was the cereal aisle that seemed to cause the most grief for me. I could not control the sudden tears that came from seeing the cheerful-looking boxes of* **Cranberry Almond Crunch** *and* **Blueberry Morning**–*Mom's favorite cereals. However, avoiding this aisle did not remedy the situation because the same embarrassing flood of tears overcame me at the table of ripe bananas in produce, the yogurt in dairy, or the cookies in the bakery aisle. These were the places where we spent many happy hours picking out things she especially liked.*

*Unlike the stock clerks in many big-city grocery stores, the friendly ones in Sedona's Safeway seem to roam the store looking for customers to help. I knew one would soon find me and offer to help. I was terrified they would ask, "Where's your mother? We haven't seen her lately." Several times I abruptly left my sparsely-filled cart and walked blindly out of the store.*

Once I understood what was happening to me, I could begin "grief work" in earnest, even as I watched my mother slowly, mysteriously dying. Oh. I never said the word *dying* before. It hurts and frightens me. I know that Alzheimer's is different with every person–Mom could spend the next 10 to 20 years slowly and painfully losing her fight for life or she could go into a rapid decline and be gone in less than two months. I would have to find ways to live my life at the same time she is losing hers, and that might be my greatest challenge . . .

### Love for $ale
*After Grace moved, I talked about having a garage sale for about four months. Finally, Josephine, a friend of mine called to inform me, "I placed an ad in the paper and your garage sale will be next week!" Then she came over and arranged and priced everything for me. I did not understand why I procrastinated until the day of the sale. I saw strangers touching and pawing through Mom's things. Suddenly I knew the reason–selling off a person's belongings is something I thought happened only* **after** *they died. I understand and accept that Grace isn't coming back to our home, but damn it, she's not dead! As people snatched up most of the things she would not need again, I numbly said "goodbye" to another part of her life.*

Finally, I accepted **relief**. Actually, this brings me right back to guilt. I refused to feel any relief about anything related to Mom and her care–I was afraid to feel joy about anything. How could I justify feeling relief while Mom was only getting worse? Somehow, I seemed to want to hold on to my pain for as long as Mom had Alzheimer's. I mistakenly thought that a loving daughter could do no less.

## *The 6th Barrier:* **KNOW-IT-ALL**

None of the people who have Alzheimer's disease today ever imagined they would be in the situation they find themselves in now. Despite current advances in medical research, no one really knows how we get Alzheimer's, who is most at risk or how to slow the disease process. Today, there is no cure. Now, that's scary.

In addition to financially supporting medical research through the Alzheimer's Association, our *words* are the most important weapon we have to fight against this disease–talking and listening–especially within our own family and circle of friends. A recent phone conversation with my sister left me marveling at just how important it is for family members to push themselves and each other beyond their familiar roles and personal comfort zones to share what they think and know. We need to express our unsure feelings and take time to listen to each other like this . . .

### Tell Me How You Really Feel

*Kay and I were casually discussing our financial plans when she said, "I'm getting prepared since I'm probably going to get 'it'." I knew 'it' was Alzheimer's. My first reaction was to make light of her comment because I was so surprised to learn that she worried about "catching" this disease. Her rationale was based on her false but firm assumption that Alzheimer's would somehow leapfrog over me, but definitely land on her!*

# Visiting Mom

*I listened without breathing as she explained that her
financial plan included a cushion to make sure she is
cared for when she gets Alzheimer's. Her words were
disturbing enough, but it was her voice that really let me
know how she felt. I could hear fear in her words and it
made me afraid, too.*

*We talked about how unpredictable the onset of
Alzheimer's is, but inheriting it has not been positively
demonstrated except in some families with early onset. It
seems my sister had been watching from the sidelines as
Mom and I struggled through each phase of the disease
with an escalating dread that she had never expressed
before. I felt terrible that I had not been more in tune
with what she might be feeling.*

*I see that months earlier I missed a cue when she
playfully assured me, "Don't worry, I'll take care of you
when the time comes." This was her mocking reminder
that she is eight years younger. Later, when I thought
about this conversation, I realized I never said the words
she probably needed to hear, "I will take care of you, too."
That's what I think she really wanted to know.*

Living with a real or imagined death sentence is no life. Kay
forced me to deal with my own fears based on what I know to
be true now. However, nothing is known today that could
prevent or cure Alzheimer's disease. I put some of Kay's
questions into a brief questionnaire for families to answer and
discuss *together*. It's called *A Family Discussion on Alzheimer's*
and can be ordered from Elder Press along with the address
for *The Five Wishes* published by Aging with Dignity.

*A Family Discussion* focuses on gaining and sharing a true understanding of Alzheimer's disease within a family unit. It is an easy and eye-opening way for families to talk about what they *think* they "know" about the disease, how it impacts mom and how each family member, including children, is responding to the challenge. It also helps with the next steps–understanding and taking responsibility for the daily care of the elder involved.

*The Five Wishes* takes the family discussion to a more personal level by asking each person to clearly define the type of care they desire in the event of their own fatal or life-threatening illness. Answering these questions for mom and for ourselves removes a tremendous burden from other family members who would otherwise have to guess the kind of care that is desired.

Words written by family and friends also have a positive effect as I learned recently when I read five very powerful words from my sister: *"You did the right thing."* That's what she wrote in her e-mail . . .

## The Right Thing
*Hi Sis,*
*I know the garage sale was difficult, but try not to feel*
*too guilty. Mom would want you to enjoy the "fruits of*
*your labors," not feel bad about them. Remember you*
*are, have been, and continue to be a loving, caring and*
*very special daughter who is doing, and has done for*
*many years, the best for her Mom. I know she feels this*
*is so even if she can't tell you. From my perspective she*
*seems to be happy and healthy, and YOU are the reason*
*she is that way.*

*I love you and appreciate ALL your efforts and many sacrifices. Hopefully, you feel I have supported you to the best of my ability. If not plz let me know what I can do that I haven't done. I luv you.     K*

Saying "You did the right thing" to family members helps to validate them and put this part of their lives into perspective. My continuing need to be reassured that I am doing what is best for Mom and for myself seems unending. Not saying this or something similar may leave family members feeling they are all alone.

Caregivers usually don't think to pat themselves on the back or even acknowledge that praise is deserved or needed. We are too busy indulging our doubts, *"Could I have kept mom a little longer?"* or *"It wasn't really that bad when I was on call 24 hours a day."* Mom is probably not able to give this type of feedback, but family members and friends can and should say what they genuinely feel. I see that within families we have to use words to express how we feel, and also ask questions and listen to other family members. This way we learn from and teach one another. It is the wisest, kindest thing we can do for mom, ourselves and our families.

## *The 7th Barrier:* **SHADOW BOXING**

How do you know if you have the right mother? I've been puzzled when friends told me they wish they had a mom like mine. I never wanted any other mother. What was wrong that would make them shop for a replacement?

I believe that each of us gets the "perfect mother" for our own growth and development–one who will help us grow into a more complete person, even when she does things we may not like. Just take one thing that you dislike about your mother and think about how that quality helped to *positively* shape who you are today. Mothers come in over 57 shades of gray between good and bad. We have the choice and the power to use each experience with or without her to create life experiences for ourselves. According to Paula Caplan in *Don't Blame Mother*, the ultimate question is: "How will you feel when your mother dies?"

This is often surprisingly different from how you feel *while* she is dying. She suggests that writing mom's biography would be a good place for each of us to start answering this question. When it is complete ask yourself how you feel about the discoveries you made about her life? What were/are your expectations and demands of her? What do you respect or regret? In the end, what really matters?

I see that having a good visit depends a lot on knowing as much about mom and our relationship as possible. It also depends on arriving at a place of peace *within* ourselves.

What often gets in the way of appreciating the mother we are given turns out to be our own myths about what our mother should be and how she should treat us. I began to see this more clearly when I read through Caplan's list of:

> Myths About Mothers
> 1. *The measure of a good mother is a perfect child.*
> 2. *Mothers are inferior to fathers.*
> 3. *Mothers are endless founts of nurturance.*
> 4. *Mothers need experts' advice to raise healthy children.*
> 5. *Mothers are bottomless pits of neediness.*
> 6. *Mothers naturally know how to raise children.*
> 7. *Mothers don't get angry.*
> 8. *Mother-child closeness is unhealthy.*
> 9. *Mothers are dangerous when they are powerful.*

Some of us find it easy to identify ways we are grateful to and for our mothers, however if you are having a hard time coming up with much to be grateful for regarding your mom, you can always, "Be grateful for all the things she didn't do!"

Dr. Susan Forward writes in her book **Toxic Parents** that, "It is not necessary to forgive your parents in order to feel better about yourself and to change your life." Too often, forgive and forget seems to really mean–*"pretend* it didn't happen." It did happen. You feel it, you remember, now it is your bitter-sweet gift. Harold Bloomfield, mentioned earlier, has also come up with a beautiful and effective way to begin to make peace with mom through writing a *Letter of Acceptance*. In this way you can experience her understanding and forgiveness–as well as yours for her. *(This letter and Bloomfield's Letter of Regrets are best accomplished in consultation with a therapist or other trained professional because of the intensity of feelings involved.)*

*Chapter 5:*
# Eight Great Habits

Practicing good visitor habits can help prevent unnecessary mental and emotional fatigue. Not knowing when or if you have *done the best you can* only creates confusion. One way to measure *your best* is to address all eight habits of a good visit. Sometimes just knowing that you covered all the bases will relieve a large part of the worry that plagues so many of us.

> **Eight Great Habits for Visitors:**
> 1. Preparation
> 2. Information Gathering
> 3. Greeting
> 4. Personal Attention
> 5. Communicating
> 6. Arts and Crafts
> 7. Physical Activities
> 8. Reassurance

Making all eight behaviors a habit is a big step toward ensuring that you and mom have the best visit possible. I was filled with questions about what I should do when I visited–how long to stay? how often to come? and so on. When I asked other visitors or staff these questions, I got a lot of vague responses like, *"You'll know."* No one seemed to have a clue. What I did discover is that *there is no single right way to visit.* This is not an exact science–visiting is an art and we are the artists. I learned many lessons from my early visits, but one of the most important was not to judge or compare what I did with what others did or did not do. . .

### Judge Not
*I arrived one day as Mom was finishing up her lunch. Suddenly a woman visitor I had not seen before walked briskly past me into the crowded resident dining room. She had a small boy in tow. They marched up to one of the men as he slowly ate his lunch and suddenly, in a loud singsong voice, she shouted, "Surprise!"*

*The man's eyes never focused on her, but he clearly recognized the little boy right away and smiled broadly. The three of them followed Mom and I out to the patio and sat nearby. I could hear the woman talking about the "air conditioner system at home." Well, after about 30 minutes of "air conditioner" talk, they went back inside.*

*The warm afternoon sun drove Mom and me inside about five minutes later. I was surprised to see the nice man slumped on a bench just outside the door–he was sleeping and he was alone. At that moment an aide passed by and said, "I guess he's all tuckered out from his wife's visit. She comes to see him twice a year!"*

I was ready to silently condemn the woman for neglecting the *nice* man when I caught myself. What do I know about them or their situation? Nothing. There could be good reasons for her bi-annual visits or there could be no reason, but really, it was none of my business.

There are so many different experiences between caregivers and people with Alzheimer's disease, and certainly between husbands and wives with or without this disease.

*Don't judge or condemn yourself or others.*

Sometime later I heard that this couple was divorced, but she continues to bring the grandchildren to see their grandfather. This incident again caused me to wonder: *What makes a visit "good"?*

About this time I discovered I had set up a dismal no-win situation for myself. I had secret and impossible-to-achieve visiting standards–I thought a *good* visit would happen only *if* Mom got well (cured of Alzheimer's) by the end of our time together *that* day. With this as my only ideal, I guaranteed failure for myself.

Now, I understand that I wasn't focused on the precious time I have with Grace, but instead I was concentrating on some future fantasy. In my delusion, I was responsible for making her well–for saving my mother! I now see both of us as winners. I don't rule out the distant possibility that she may be cured completely–that would surely be a gift, but it is not the only gift–it may not even be the best gift because . . .

*Each moment I have with her is a gift.*

*The 1st Great Habit:*
# Preparation

After only a few visits I found that visiting could be fun and interesting. I also discovered that a good visit did not have to be either fun or interesting to make it the best visit possible. The first two times I visited, I brought a few things with me: a book for us to read from and talk about; a muffin; silk flowers in a pot; and two new T-shirts–all stuffed into a plastic grocery bag. The next time I added manicure tool; curlers; a small hair dryer; and comfortable new shoes and socks. This time I carried everything in two plastic bags–ugh! This did not look cool, but it was the beginning of my idea for a Visiting Bag.

**Some basic items in my *Visiting Bag* include:**

| | |
|---|---|
| *Phone Card* | *Manicure tools* |
| *Small brush and comb* | *Small, sharp scissors* |
| *Nail polish/remover* | *Tissues (small packages)* |
| *"Handi-wipes"* | *Tweezers* |
| *Black laundry marker* | *Hand mirror/Sunglasses* |
| *Hand cream in a tube* | *Lipstick/"Chapstick"* |
| *Toothbrush/ Cup* | *"Depends" w/straps* |
| *Writing paper/pens* | *Music/cassette/CD* |
| *Travel sewing kit* | *Small books* |
| *"Treasure Book"* | *Cell phone (optional)* |

The best bag for visiting is strong, lightweight and roomy enough to hold everything you need for each trip. It is about 16"X 13" and made of sturdy nylon or canvas fabric. It is best if it has a zipper opening so the contents won't spill out in the car trunk.

After only two visits Mom caught on that when I came, I would have a *treat* for her in my visiting bag. I started putting her treats–usually a piece of fresh fruit or a muffin or cookie–into a separate small, brightly-colored bag to make it easy for her to find. She recognizes the Visiting Bag right away, so I give her a separate Treat Bag to carry. As soon as we are seated, she reaches in to get her treat. Her eyes twinkle because she knows *it* is waiting for her. She lets me know she wants *it* by signaling with her hand while she looks expectantly at me. Sometimes she prompts me with, *"Where's the good stuff?"*

There is no such thing as going to see "just one person" in a nursing home. It is best to be prepared to meet, greet and treat–with personal attention or a piece of candy–five or more residents before you leave. I put a few pieces of wrapped hard candy in my pocket when I visit for some of the residents who greet me in the hallways. Sometimes a piece of candy is also a last treat for Mom just before I leave. I learned right away that it is best not to arrive empty-handed. Keep your Visiting Bag in your car trunk or someplace else where it is handy.

*The 2nd Great Habit:*
# Information Gathering

When I reach the nurse's station I briefly speak to the nurse or aide on duty and ask about Grace. I want to know about anything that might have happened since my last visit or phone call. This small act however, is not always as simple and clear cut as it may seem.

When I ask, "How's my Mom doing?", the usual answer is: *"She's doing 'good'."* I discovered that the words *fine* and *good* may have several different meanings when spoken by professional caregivers. Staff responses may actually mean:

> *"She hasn't done anything that I know about today."*
> *"Nothing unusual happened on my shift."*
> *"She went to the bathroom on schedule."*
> *"She has been very sweet (quiet) lately."*

The staff response could also mean any number of other things that reflect *their* work schedule, shift changes and staffing levels rather than what I think they mean. When visitors ask questions we usually want to know much more than we actually put into words. What we really want to know about mom is similar, but necessarily different from what concerns professional staff. We really want to know:

> *"Is she happy?"*
> *"Does she sleep peacefully?"*
> *"Has she made any real friends yet?"*
> *"Does she like it here?"*

These are things most staff members do not know. They answer from their perspective, as professional full-time caregivers, and that is as it should be. It is up to us, the family and friends, to take our concerns to the next level and ask more specific questions, like:

> *"Is she getting iced water with her lunch every day?"*
> *"What did the doctor report about her foot pain?"*
> *"How often does she go to the bathroom at night?"*
> *"Does she participate in the morning exercises?"*

When I am satisfied with the answers I get from staff, I use that information to help guide what we choose to do or not do during my time with Grace that day. At the end of our visit, I sometimes have additional questions to ask the nurses. Whenever they do something that is generous, kind or thoughtful, I comment and tell them how much Grace and I appreciate their care.

*The 3rd Great Habit:*

## Give a Warm Greeting

Greeting mom means more that just saying the words, *"Hi, Mom."* This part of the visit actually starts when I open the door to the nursing home and say *"Hello"* to each of the residents who greet me. I can do this now with ease, but at first, it was very difficult for me. Now, I make eye contact often and smile before moving on to Grace's room. I also make a point of stopping briefly and talking to one or two residents during each visit. I call as many people by their name as possible and avoid asking them, *"How are you?"* I learned a hard and unforgettable lesson about mindlessly greeting residents with that commonly acceptable question . .

### How Are You Today?
*One day I greeted a usually cheerful and chatty resident with this innocent question. She abruptly replied,*
***"I just feel like killing myself and dying! Ya know***
***what I mean, honey?"** I realized that my other*
*unthinking greeting, "Have a nice day" was not going to*
*work either. I stopped walking, held her hand and asked,*

*"Has something happened lately to make you feel this way?" She said, "I just get this way sometimes, but I do want to just lay down and die . . . (sigh) I'll be myself again. I'll be better the next time you come."*

*Before I left that day I talked to the nurse about what this lady said. I asked if they knew what was going on with her. They did not know but said they would talk with her to find out what they could.*

Well, what do you say instead of "How are you?" Unless I am prepared to spend time with one of the residents, I don't ask a question at all. Instead, I find something specific about them I can comment or compliment them on, for instance:

*"Hi, I really like your new hair cut."*
*"Oh good, you finally got that cast off your foot!"*
*"It's good to see you today, I missed you last week."*

Then I go on to Grace's room. She still recognizes me so I have the pleasure of seeing joy on her face as soon as she sees me. I want to remember that look forever. It tells me who I am, where I come from. I hug and kiss her and tell her how glad I am to see her. Then I take her other hand as we slowly walk outside to the patio or into the living room, or sometimes we stay in her room for our visit.

At the beginning of this chapter I mentioned *"Hi, Mom"* as a greeting, but on days when Mom is more confused than others, she may not respond to *"Mom"* and I call her by her given name, Grace.

### Gracious!

*Just before we moved to Arizona, I took Mom to the beauty shop for her regular monthly appointment. I had recently started calling her "Grace" when I wanted to get her attention but especially since she had started calling me "Mom." I talked her through each step with the stylist: "Grace, come and sit over here . . . Do you want some Pepsi? . . Grace, do you like this hair cut?"*

*After he finished, the stylist leaned over to me and in a stage whisper that held the faintest hint of disapproval, said, "I thought she was your mother!" I replied, "She is." "But, you call her by her first name!" I suppressed a smile and told him, "I use her name so she'll know I'm talking to her." His eyes widened and he slowly nodded his approval and understanding.*

Each person's name is very important to them and especially to a person with Alzheimer's. I first understood this several years ago when I introduced Grace to some of my friends from work. They were all between 40 and 60 years of age. I introduced her as *"My mother, Grace"* and they referred to her as Grace for the rest of the evening. That night after everyone was gone, she firmly told me, *"I would prefer that they call me 'Mrs. Thomas' and not be so familiar!"* This was how my friends addressed her when we were all a lot younger.

I have also had to correct some of the staff in the nursing home. The popular and friendly custom many young people have today is to give everyone they like a nickname, sometimes just a twist of their real name. This does not work well on people with Alzheimer's. Grace does not like to be called "*Gracie.*" Changing her name is not an act of friendship to her. It is a sign of disrespect and who knows where it will lead? So I have asked staff just to call her "*Grace.*"

## *Hugging*

I found another great way to greet Grace–with touch. When I hug her, I hold and embrace her. I also hold her hand a lot. I think the way we hug, kiss and hold hands tells as much about us as handshakes are supposed to reveal about how we will conduct business. I've observed hugs that are popular, but somehow seem lacking in warmth. I've also witnessed one hug that seems to warm just about everyone...

> **The Indigestion Hug**–*This is when adults put their arms around one another and vigorously slap or pat the other person on the back. I always wonder if they think the other person needs to burp. I guess some people must like this hug, but we don't.*

> **The Time's Up Hug**–*Similar to the indigestion hug, but different. These hugs get off to a good start by warmly holding mom in an embrace, but suddenly something happens. I don't know what happens, but it seems as if a hugging stopwatch goes off and mom is given a final squeeze that clearly says, "Enough, time is up!"*

> **The Teflon Hug**–*This non-stick hug is accomplished by leaning toward mom like a real hug is about to occur, but just before physical contact takes place, the visitor grabs mom's arm and holds her off at a distance. It's as though the visitor has a fear that he or she might actually come in contact with mom or catch something.*

'Til She Gets Enough Hug–*This is the best kind of
hug for mom. It happens when you let her stop hugging
first. Grace loves to be hugged and I found she wants to
be held longer that I usually hug. One day I started
letting her decide how much hugging she wanted and she
seemed much more satisfied. When we finish hugging, I
look in her eyes and tell her, "I love you." Then I gently
squeeze her hands.*

## Kissing

Talking about kissing mom seems to embarrass a lot of
people. I think of kissing as one of the highest forms of affection and not reserved just for romantic occasions. When I visit
Grace I want her to know I care about her. Every family has
its own language for showing affection, but if you are not
satisfied with your usual family-style greeting, you can start
giving mom what you think she would like to receive.

My Mom, sister and I kiss each other lightly on the lips
followed by a "real" hug. What determines a good or bad kiss
actually depends on agreement and acceptance between the
kissers. Here are some examples of kisses I've seen lately. The
last kiss called "golden" is one that even an outsider can see is
a sign of mutual love and affection.

Airy Fairy Kisses–*These seem to blow right by mom's
cheek and miss her altogether. Usually part of a "Teflon
Hug," these so-called kisses are reserved for mothers we
don't want to touch or have touch us–especially not with
their lips.*

**Kentucky-fried Kisses**–*Men seem to do this more than women. I'm talking about the kind of lip-smacking sound I frequently hear from people enjoying fried chicken. Mom is not a drumstick!*

**Gone-With-the-Wind Kisses**–*These are kisses that you blow off your palm. They are supposed to float toward mom. I wonder how many people actually like to be on the receiving end of this kind of kiss? O.K., maybe as you say good-bye, but not in place of a real kiss.*

**Zorro Kisses**–*These leave their mark on mom's cheek. Who wants to walk around with lip imprints on their cheeks? If you happen to leave your mark, be sure to gently wipe it off as soon as possible. You may erase your lipstick from her face, but you will still leave your mark on her heart.*

**Golden Kisses**–*Clearly transmit love and affection. I have an old photo of Grace reuniting with her much-loved 99 year-old aunt whom she had not seen for over fifty years. Aunt Alice lived in a nursing home and came for a brief appearance at our first family reunion in her town. As Grace gently kissed her on the cheek, Aunt Alice placed her hand on her face and softly held it there as they tearfully smiled into each other's eyes.*

### The Eyes Have It

Each of our senses is important, but I have never been so aware of them as I am now that Mom is steadily losing hers. I am most consciously thankful for her good eyesight now.

Eye contact shows that I actually see and experience Grace and it gives her a chance to look at me. Sitting at her eye-level when we are together is important to clear communication. Each visit I make sure she has a chance to look in her mirror to check her hair or makeup. This way she can look at her own face and maybe recognize it for a little while longer.

When Grace searches my eyes, I think she looks for what means the most to her these days, to feel loved and deeply connected to me. She seeks out my eyes and seems to rest there for the briefest second. When I look into her eyes I am a child again. I know she can see that I still need her comfort, even as I am there to comfort her. She can also see the anxiety and turmoil I experience. Even though I try to rid myself of it before I see her, I know she can see inside my heart. What I see in her eyes is enough to keep me going.

*The 4th Great Habit:*
# Personal Care

The first second I see Grace, I give her personal attention. I look her over quickly and look into her eyes to see the unspoken answer to my question, *"How are you today, Mom?"* I somewhat casually check her arms and legs for any signs of bruising–just in case. This is also the time I *casually* glance around her room to see if it is clean and orderly and that most of her belongings are there.

I also look at what Mom is wearing, the condition of her nails and hair. I want to know that she is being cared for properly. Grace would have a hard time dressing herself these days if she had to do it alone, so my help and the daily help of the staff at the nursing home is needed to complete this very basic task.

Today when I visited, I was dismayed to find that her jeans were very wrinkled and ragged strings were trailing behind her from the hem of her pants legs. It did not occur to me when she first moved there that the laundry service would not *iron* clothes for the residents. However, most of the time her clothes had been folded or hung so there were few noticeable wrinkles. But now five pairs of recently purchased jeans have been torn or cut in some way–just in the last six months!

When Grace moved in I was given three laundry options:
1) Use the facility laundry services included in her monthly fees; 2) Pay $20 per month extra for a private laundry service run by an aide; or 3) Wash the clothes myself. Washing and ironing have never been at the top of my list of things I want to do. Before moving Mom, ironing simply did not happen, in fact I can't even find my iron. Picking Option #1 was easy, but now I'm paying the price. I am going to try Option #2 for a while.

## The Glamour Police

Mom's curly hair seems to grow by leaps and bounds since she has been in the nursing home. Her hair isn't exactly wash-and-wear so I cut it shorter, thinking it would look better after it was wet. Finally, I decided to try the on-site beautician although Mom is very fussy about her hair. I held my breath and hoped this would be a positive experience–for both of them. I sighed with relief when I found out every-thing went remarkably well.

DeeDee, the nursing home beautician is very patient and seems perfectly suited to meet the needs and temperaments of the elderly residents. She has a wide range of practical hair cuts and styles that help residents remember themselves at their best in a 1950-ish style, or something more up-to-date. I can see that styling hair for a culturally diverse population of women between 70 to 100 years of age is quite a feat.

### The Bathroom

For most adults going to the toilet is a private matter. But when Alzheimer's strikes, what normally happened only behind closed doors suddenly becomes embarrassingly public. Being sensitive to a total change in the way Grace has to use the bathroom is important to her well being. Most of us use the toilet alone but now, Mom almost always has an aide in there with her–the entire time. Try to imagine what it would be like to have a stranger (probably a young woman) take you to the bathroom. . .

### Imagine
*"Let's go to the potty."*
*What's that? Why is the girl unbuttoning my pants?*
*"Stop that!"*
*Now she's pulling down my underpants (diaper)!*
*"NO!"*
*What is she going to do to me? Oh, I know what she's up to. I can pull my own pants down, thank you. The girl is just standing there. I better hurry up. I want her to leave! She keeps saying, "Go to the bathroom." Where is it? Should I go now? I'm trying to hurry up but nothing happens!*
*"Pppppusssh!"*

*What does she mean? Push what? Oops! Good,*
*something happened.*
"*Let me wipe you.*"
*Is she nuts?*
"*NO! Give me the paper.*"
*I can do it myself, thank you very much. Who is she?*
*I need some help!*
"*Here, girl, you take this paper.*"
*Now she's pulling on my pants again.*
"*I want to keep my pants. Leave me alone!*"

Going to the toilet gives me another opportunity to monitor mom's health. Parents of new babies do this all the time—it isn't especially pleasant then and it sure isn't fun when it's your own mother. I always say, "*You don't have to hurry, Mom, take all the time you need.*"

As I help Grace off the toilet seat, I discreetly check the color of her urine or the consistency of her stool. Recent research shows just how important it is to be aware of color changes. If I notice a change, I contact the nurse to discuss whether there is a need for medical attention. Grace is not incontinent, but she does have trouble remembering where the bathroom is at night.

Recently I discovered that the word "*toilet*" has disappeared from Grace's vocabulary. She no longer connects the word *toilet* to anything, even when she is sitting on it. She doesn't know what it is or where to look for it. I haven't figured out what to call "*it*" yet, but I found out that telling her to, "*Put the paper in there,*" and pointing just wasn't clear enough. She never used the words *potty* or *john*, so I'm going to ask her to rename it. Right now she calls it, "*This?*" And so it is.

*The 5th Great Habit:*
# Communicating

Communication with Grace is so different now compared to all the years before Alzheimer's or even last year, and there are several important differences to be aware of during our visits. I try to let her say anything she wants first, before I talk. She rarely initiates conversation, but she pays attention to what is said and makes every effort to respond and participate. My job is to make it as easy as possible for her to talk to me and to say things to her in ways she can easily understand.

Liz Ayres, a volunteer and former caregiver, created a helpful handout that highlights effective ways to communicate with people with Alzheimer's disease. I adapted some of them to fit visiting situations. Below are some important things *not* to say or do when you are with mom.

**Don't use logic, reason or common sense.**
Logic does not work with people who have Alzheimer's. This is hard for caregivers to remember. We seem to revert to logic when we are really tired and cranky, but it doesn't make sense to her now. Be creative and adjust to her ability level–even if it doesn't exactly make sense to you.

**Don't argue.**
Agree as much as possible or distract her by switching to another subject or activity. Try leaving the room to avoid being involved in heated debates.

**Don't confront her with *your* facts.**
Accept the blame when something goes wrong (even
if it's a fantasy to you). Use words like "it", "them"
and "they" to comment on what mom has said,
especially when you are not sure what she is talking
about.

**Don't remind her that she forgets.**
When she asks you to repeat what you said, use
exactly the same words in the same way when you
do. Speak to her in short, one-sentence statements.
Try to use words with no more than three syllables.
Mom will be less anxious if you talk about things
that are happening today, right now. Avoid asking
her if she "remembers" anything.

I learned many of these tips before I moved Mom and now
they are a natural way for me to communicate. They also
work well with people who don't have Alzheimer's! As
helpful as all this information is, it is not everything I need to
know to talk with her now.

### Two-way communication

I found I have to allow more time and opportunities for each
of us to speak and listen to one another. In Naomi Feil's
book, *The Validation Breakthrough,* she spells out some of the
most effective techniques available today that increase our
ability to communicate to people with Alzheimer's. I strongly
recommend her book to every family caring for someone with
this disease. I was able to apply what I learned immediately
and improve our talks.

*Eight Great Habits*

## What to Say When You Visit

I had not given much thought about just how different it is talking to a person who can't remember much of their past–sometimes, they can't remember or say their own name. This loss of memory greatly changes and limits my usual choice of conversation topics. So, I put together several of the basic things I say during a regular visit.

*"Hi Mom, it's me, Sherry."*
Introducing myself to my own mother is strange and painful but it sure helps get each visit off to a smooth start. This greeting takes a lot of the confusion and guesswork out of the first few moments and helps to put her at ease.

*"You look very pretty today."*
Mom likes to receive compliments and she looks forward to hearing something nice about herself from me each time I visit. Sometimes I tell her a short story about a time when she wore something similar to what she has on and how great she looks today.

*"How are you feeling?"*
Mom usually says "fine," but sometimes she seems to be thinking about her answer. That usually means that she might have something that she is trying to remember to tell me about how she is feeling. When she hesitates, I ask her several questions about headaches, arthritis in her fingers, stomach ache, scratches, etc. as we look over each part of her body that we discuss. She likes the attention. Once in a while she remembers something that hurt.

*"Show me your room."*
Grace usually doesn't know which way to go to her
room, but she is more than willing to try to find it.
She does not want me to know that she doesn't
know her own room, so she gets busy looking in all
directions. For the first few months she had trouble
going to the right room because she was identifying
her room as a room that had a dresser in it. She
didn't realize that every room had the same kind of
furniture. I began helping her find "her" room by
looking for her blue-flowered bedspread. When we
find it she is very proud and says, "This is *my* room."

*"Is your food good?"*
This probably sounds like a boring question, but
knowing how well Grace enjoys her food is very
important. I ask about each item on her plate and
that way I get an idea about how her taste buds are
working. Sometimes she says the food has "No
taste–ugh!" This means that it needs either a little
salt or sugar. When we are eating, I sometimes talk
about special meals she has fixed for us in the past. I
relate my story to the foods she has in front of her
and she enjoys hearing about her starring role in my
memories of her.

*"Let's read your Treasure Book for a while."*
Grace is very agreeable and interested in doing
different things and going to new places. However,
few things hold her interest for more than five
minutes at a time. Reading to her means having
pictures or photos to look at or maybe reading two
or three lines of a poem or story.

*"I love you, Mom."*
I always tell her this during our visit and always as I am leaving. I don't remember telling her that I loved her much while I was growing up. I remember buying greeting cards that said *it* for me. Now it feels natural for both of us to say and hear these words. I probably could never say this too often.

*"I have to go now, but I'll be back in two days."*
Telling Grace that I will be back soon is important for her to know. At first I only said, "I have to go now" and she always asked me "if" I was coming back and "when" I would return to see her. Sometimes she delays parting just a bit by asking me more about what I will be doing when I'm away from her. This is the time when *it is so important not to rush.*

We went through one period when Mom had to have everything, and I mean everything, repeated twice. I never knew if I needed to talk louder or if the words sounded blurred when they got to her ears. I had her hearing checked, but it was fine. After a while she did not need things repeated, but I never knew what caused this to happen.

Talking louder did not seem to stop her from asking, *"What did you say?"* A few times I got impatient and said, *"Mom, I already told you one hundred times!"* Then she would look right at me and in a calm voice say, *"Well, tell me one hundred and one times!"* This always cracked me up and of course reminded me which one of us was the "mother." Speaking slower did seem to help and I also started speaking in shorter sentences. These techniques still work well today.

## *Silence*

Our conversations get shorter and shorter, but I sometimes find that I still do too much talking. I thought that we couldn't just sit there and say nothing, could we? Yes, we can, and sometimes now, we do. Silence is necessary when we are together because Grace tries hard to think of things to say. Occasionally, she really concentrates and even remembers some of what she thought about at an earlier time. It was something that she really wanted to say to me, not earth-shaking, but important enough to bring up when we are together. *"I wanted to ask you something, it was about . . .I know it was important . . .Oh, it'll come back to me . . .it had to do with–my hair, that's it!"* My heart breaks when I hear all the effort it takes her to say this. I'm reminded once again that Grace knows she is losing her abilities and yet she quietly fights to maintain all that she can.

## *Questions*

One of the short-cuts to talking with Mom turned out to have a surprisingly negative effect on our ability to communicate–asking a bunch of questions. *"Just who do you think you are, the FBI?"* That's what Grace asked me once when she thought I was asking too many questions. Of course she gave me short, terse answers and soon both of us were crabby.

I remembered an important lesson from my college days about asking questions: they put many people on the defensive. This is the last thing I wanted to do to Mom. When I ask her questions, she usually has to remember something in order to respond to even the simplest query. When she can't remember, she is reminded again that she has lots of trouble keeping track of things, that she is worried about possibly being crazy or that she may be losing her mind. On a good day, she knows that she does not know where she is. I try not to put her in this frightening and humiliating position.

## *Listening*

Listening to Mom requires more than just hearing the words that she says. It means listening with my eyes and my heart as well as with my ears. Her vocabulary is really quite small now. In fact, the word *"small"* gets substituted for several other words when she means cold, hot, up, down, big, loud, not-sweet-enough, etc. Sometimes I question her just so I can better understand what she is talking about and sometimes she doesn't like that at all. She gets irritated when she knows she did not use the right word.

Several of my friends have seen me talking with Grace and they comment that, *"You are so lucky to be able to talk with your Mom. My mother doesn't talk to me at all."* I can feel the pain that comes when they speak these words and I hold my breath. I wonder how much longer we will be able to talk to each other. Many of the residents have much greater difficulty talking and communicating than Mom does. I can only guess what it is like to visit someone who does not talk or respond—many of us will find out.

A few residents start off speaking clearly and get out a few words that make perfect sense, when suddenly they start talking gibberish. I used to wonder what *gibberish* sounded like, but now that I know, the word needs no further explanation. Gibberish is exactly like it sounds.

### Say What?

*The other day a sweet lady stopped me in the hallway to Grace's room. She very clearly said, "Wait a minute, can I show you something?" I went over to look at what she was pointing to on the cover of a magazine in her hand. She said, "I was looking at this …bub-a-lub." Huh? "Bub-a-bub-boom-bleepedity-boom!" she exclaimed. All the while she was pointing to various things on the cover. She clearly wanted to talk about something that she saw there.*

*I sat down next to her as she continued telling me something in total gibberish. Then I told her, "I agree and think it's a good thing. I have to go now, but I'll see you later." She seemed to understand me and responded with, "Bibbety boom." I think I began to understand her, too.*

### *Three-way Communication*

Talking with Grace, the staff and aides is important. Occasionally, I talk to staff with Mom present. It helps her understand how I feel and interact with them and helps to set the tone for how she feels about talking with them when she has a concern. I make sure she is with me when I talk to them about something that worried her. This validates her concern and she feels all of us are paying attention to her needs. I also make sure that no one talks "about" her when she is present. I only have to say once, *"Speak directly to Grace"* to get the message across. Sometimes when more than one person is talking, Mom has trouble following the conversation. I explain what is being said as I gently hold her hand or arm, look into her eyes and wait for her to focus. I use short sentences. I don't use baby talk.

Grace is very aware that she has trouble participating in conversations. I see her straining to conceal her frustration. Sometimes she seems to *try* harder, but other times she just shuts down and talks a lot less than she would like. I make it easier for her when I slow the pace of the conversation and use shorter sentences. I want her to feel as *normal* as possible for as long as I can. Grace taught me a little about how it feels to be ignored and treated as if we have lost our mind–it makes a person feel sad and humiliated. Mom described exactly how she felt when she tried to talk to an older neighbor woman.

## She Talked Too Much!

*When we still lived in Michigan, one of our neighbors invited Grace to visit her own mother who was wheelchair-bound. Mom liked the idea of getting to know someone close by who was near her age. She did not hesitate to visit. I was very happy that she wanted to make a new friend.*

*Unfortunately I discovered this did not happen. Mom returned home about an hour later. She was spitting and fuming as she came through the door. I couldn't imagine what had upset her and asked her, "What on earth happened?" "The daughter wouldn't let her mother talk!" she blurted out. "Every single time I said something or asked the woman anything, the daughter was sitting right there and answered before the mother had a chance to open her mouth. She never had a chance to say anything! "The only words the poor woman got out were to ask me, 'Do you go to church?' I could see that she wanted to talk about this, but the daughter wouldn't let her. I never got a chance to answer before that daughter started talking again. I don't want to go back there. It was terrible!!"*

I thought I learned from Grace's frustrating experience, but recently, I found myself doing almost the same thing with one of her friends. Sometimes it takes her a while to answer questions from other people. I was trying to save her from embarrassment as she tried to answer the simple question, *"Where did you used to live?"* When she can't remember or doesn't know an answer, she usually looks to me to answer for her. It is hard to tell when to jump in and speak for her and when to let her take her time and try to come up with her own response. I want her to talk for as long as possible, so I hesitate more and make sure she knows that whatever she says is *all right.*

Sometimes Mom's words just won't come out right. She gets stuck on repeating a word that doesn't make sense to either of us. *"Take the doggle and put it away."* The doggle. Doggle? I try to figure out what this new word could possibly mean, but I'm not always successful and that frustrates both of us. When this happens, I usually just use the new word in a humorous way, add it to our vocabulary and even make up additional nonsense words.

I understand that Mom probably will talk less and less as time goes on. Soon, too soon, she may not speak at all. When and if this happens, I hope she will be comforted just to hear me–the feeling behind my words, the caring sound of my voice. I want her to see a loving reflection of all that she is as we continue to celebrate her life. When we visit mom or any elder with a disease like Alzheimer's, talking with them about the wonderful, fun, interesting and important things they have done and continue to do is a big part of our conversation.

Mothers need to feel that they are is loved, cared for and safe. They still want to *give* love and to feel needed and appreciated. We can help them express their thoughts and feelings, joys and fears . . . even as we express ours to them.

*The 6th Great Habit:*

# Encourage Arts and Crafts

I'm not an actress, singer or musician, so the idea of *entertaining* another adult is foreign to me–especially my own mother. Just what could I possibly do to entertain her? I finally answered this question when I learned to engage Grace in activities that stimulate her mind, body and spirit and end up bringing her joy, if only for a moment. She may not remember much of what we did, but she knows what is happening while it is occurring.

Please see the next chapter, *Five Fun Activities* for ideas and instructions on creative ways to have fun with mom. The basic activities are not fancy, they engage both of you in everyday activities like reading, talking, singing, laughing and celebrating.

*The 7th Great Habit:*

# Physical Activities

Getting physical with mom requires special attention for several reasons. One is that we all come from a different generation than she does. This difference really shows up because of the very different ideas about what physical activities are appropriate or even fun. In fact the idea of physical activities as something *interesting* is even in question.

Recently, I discovered that my idea about what Grace *needed* was at odds with what she *wanted.* I arranged for my fantastic massage therapist to visit her in the nursing home for a relaxing massage. I was so pleased with myself for coming up with such a creative idea. I imagined how great she would feel after all those knotted muscles were relaxed and soothed. But this was not to be. Even though I was right there with her, Grace did not like the idea of a stranger touching and rubbing her naked back. She was just about to become *crabby* when I stopped the massage and we went for a walk instead. I realized that Mom had never had a massage before. She never went to a spa either. This misadventure seemed to add tension rather than release it as I had planned. This was my idea of a good time, not hers.

I traced the root of my great massage idea back to my childhood years. Mom used to tell us to *"Give something you would like for yourself."* Well, I did that and now look what happened. My new, enlightened gift-giving motto is: **"Give or do something mom would like."**

I wasn't ready to give up completely on massage because I know how critical "touch" is to everyone. I touch Grace almost all the time we are together. I let my hands say what my words can't. I give her back massages that she can enjoy. This is done without the big announcement: "This is a *massage.*" I found out I was even using the wrong word. *"Rub"* is the correct term–she grew up with *rub* and understands what it means.

Today, I find several quiet ways to touch her and I use one or more techniques during each visit. I gently rub her arm as we sit side-by-side; hold her hand and rub the back of her palm; rub her feet, toes and ankles after I clip her toenails; give her a neck and shoulder rub; or use soothing circular motions to slowly *scratch* her back. This is a real treat for her and one of the things I do near the end of our time together. She finds this very relaxing.

## *Day-tripping*

Taking Grace out of the nursing home gives her a refreshing break from her daily life and activities. This is also something *I know* she enjoys. We make regular walking trips in the grocery store, eat in nearby restaurants, tour outdoor art fairs and window shop in the mini-malls. All of these are activities we enjoyed together for many years. Mom rarely remembers anything about our trips–once she turns her back the memory is gone. However, she does know that I am doing something with her and that is what is important to her.

Just before we leave the nursing home, I get her to "try" to use the bathroom. This approach usually produces good results and we don't have to deal with public restrooms on our trip. Men, especially, have to plan this part of the outing carefully because bathroom breaks for mom must be included. If possible, come with a female visitor to help mom use the toilet–asking a stranger to take mom to the bathroom is not an option.

When Grace and I are out, I make sure she gets plenty of rest breaks. We sit down and casually observe and comment on whatever is going on around us. Many stores do not have chairs for customers, but every store manager I have asked has quickly produced a chair for Mom. These frequent stops allow us to have a longer outing without making her too tired.

Grace usually finds something she wants to *buy* when we shop. In the grocery store, I do my regular shopping for the week and she puts her choices in the cart, too. This is usually not much, but if she goes overboard, like picking three packs of cookies *and* two cakes, I discreetly take them out of the cart when she is not looking.

### Another Beautiful Blue Blouse
*When we go to retail malls, Grace likes to carry her new purchase as we continue walking from store to store. As we stroll along, she is frequently surprised to find she is holding an unfamiliar bag. She asks me, "What's in here?" We find a place to sit down so she can open the bag. When she looks inside, she always gets a jolt of pleasure as she discovers her "beautiful blue blouse" once again. She doesn't remember buying it or discovering it just ten minutes earlier. It's worth every penny to see the look of joy on her face, even for just a fleeting moment.*

### Dining Pleasures

I learned to forget about table manners and just let Grace *eat, drink and be merry!* I take her out to nearby restaurants about once a week. We try to arrive in between popular meal times when there are the least number of customers–noisy crowds are distracting and make her anxious. Picking out something on the menu is too confusing and difficult for her–there are just too many choices and decisions to make and the words are too difficult for her to read. I usually pick out two dishes I think she would like and we discuss her selection from these two options. I show her the final choice on the menu and she can read a few words out loud. This way she still has a say about what she eats.

I learned some time ago what will happen when Grace exclaims, *"My food doesn't have any taste!"* She will complain about it repeatedly until *my* food doesn't have any taste either. There has to be some kind of sweet taste or a very mild spicy taste to most of her dishes. Our dining goal is to find a restaurant with recognizable, tasty food. When she remembers being in the restaurant before, she says, *"We have a good time here."*

Grace still has a lot of her very proper table manners, but they are losing ground to some new ones. She likes to use her fingers to pick up food much more than usual. She cleans the food off them in the best *"finger-licking-good"* manner possible because her napkin is reserved for the very end of the meal. I take *Handi-wipes* along to help her clean up.

She has developed some new out-of-the-box eating habits that are quite intriguing. I'm always amazed at some of her unique food combinations. Recently I held my breath as she topped her steamed spinach with a little lemon meringue pie! Then there was the time she sprinkled some chopped green onions over the whipped cream of her strawberry shortcake, *"For color–yum!"* These unusual food combinations look terrible to me, but they are a delicious surprise to her.

Not everyone appreciates these precious eating habits. When we go to a restaurant, I try to find a *"quiet table"* for our meal. This is important since I never know when Mom might suddenly pop her teeth out to clean them. She can do this without causing other diners to suddenly jump up and run out of the restaurant, if I choose a quiet table. Most of my visits start just before Grace's lunch time. When it is warm, we take her lunch out in the courtyard where it's quiet.

### Exercising

As important as it is to understand that each generation has preferences, Grace also taught me a lesson about individual differences, especially related to physical exercise. The conversation snipets below are good examples of how attitudes and activities have changed over the years and from person to person, for example . . .

> "A *brisk* walk is what we need." *(Fast is good)*
> *"It's not ladylike to get all sweaty."*
> "I'll buy you some nice Nikes." *(They're the coolest)*
> *"Thank you, but what's that?"*
> "Let's start walking five days a week." *(More is better)*
> *"Are we in a race or something?"*
> "Wow, we walked farther than ever!" *(A personal best)*
> *("I think my daughter needs a hobby!")*

These days walking starts when I take Mom's hand and gently help her out of her chair. I hold her hand and let her take my arm if she wants. I was slow in realizing her increasing need to physically depend on me, but I learned.

## Walk This Way

*It took some time for me to understand why Grace used
to always walk one or two steps behind me. It didn't
matter how slowly I walked, she would always stay
behind me. One day, I simply asked her, "Mom, why do
you always walk behind me?" She nonchalantly
answered, "It's a good way for me to know which way to
go." Why didn't I think of that? This is how I finally
started to hold her hand whenever we went out. She
likes this too because it takes so much of the guesswork
out of trying to follow me and she can relax more.*

Of course not every mom is able to walk with ease or to walk
at all. Physical exercise for our elders takes on new meaning
and covers much more than we may have originally thought.
Everyone requires regular exercise to maintain overall health
and well being. We have to find out how to assist mom and
participate with her. Touch, *our* touch is essential. Find out
what is appropriate for this time in her life and explore everything that is available wherever she lives now.

*The 8th Great Habit:*
# Reassure Before Leaving

What I do and say when it's time for me to leave is very
important to both of us, but for different reasons. Grace's
immediate and lasting need is to feel secure that my leaving
is only "temporary" and that I will come to see her again very
soon. Her fear is that I will not return, that she won't see me
again, that she will be left alone. I know this because she told
me once.

My own fears rise up to meet hers.  Saying goodbye to her is very hard for me too because I don't want to leave her there, I want her with me.  Grace doesn't cling to me or plead to go with me.  She trusts me to come back as I say I will.  That's what I tell her, *"I've got to go for now, but I'll be back in two days."* She asks for reassurance, *"Two days?"*
*"Yes,"* I say, *"I'll be back in two days, just like the last time."*
*"Two days?"* she repeats.
*"Yes, just two days. I'll be back and we'll go out to lunch and have a good time, O.K.? I love you, Mom."*

When it's time to leave, I make sure I am sitting down to say our farewells.  I believe the body language of standing makes it seem like I want to rush out of the room or that I've got some place else to go.  When I'm with her, I want her to feel what I feel. . .

*There is no place else I'd rather be than with her.*

*Chapter 6:*
# Five Arts and Crafts

After all the feeding, dressing and housekeeping for Grace, arts and crafts projects are the fun part of many of our visits. That doesn't mean there is no work or preparation for our activities, but it is less intense and usually ends up with mutually enjoyable results. Arts and Crafts activities are *basic* visiting tools. Five that I use are listed below and briefly discussed on the next few pages.

1. **Reading** – *stories, inspiration/religious, news*
2. **Laughing** – *jokes, poems, cartoons, funny stories*
3. **Making Music** – *singing, listening, playing*
4. **Storytelling** – *family tales, personal stories*
5. **Celebrating** – *holidays, birthdays, any day*

Quite a few visitors, however, tell me this is probably the most stressful part of their visit and they try to avoid it completely. Helping an elder with arts and crafts requires some creativity and many visitors are just plain tired, with little energy left over to give to these activities.

In this part of our visit, I make an extra effort to "create joy" for Grace–it gives us both energy. Usually it takes no more than 15 minutes of our time together, but even five special minutes of arts and crafts is refreshing and fun.

I learned some interesting things about Alzheimer's that help me understand what elders may or may not experience at the mere mention of *fun* or *arts and crafts*. For example, this disease affects each person's brain and body differently and there is **no predictable pattern** of progression for everybody. Various mental and/or physical functions may rapidly change and deteriorate while others mysteriously seem to remain intact. These variables help explain why some elders might respond in surprising ways to different activities:

1. *She may **not remember** activities she used to enjoy,.*
   *or she may remember, but **have difficulty** doing*
   *things that once seemed automatic.*
2. *Mom may **lose interest** in completing even the*
   *smallest part of an activity.*
3. *She may **not want to do** the activity at all or*
   *just not right now. The activity may seem **too***
   ***childish.***
4. *The activity may seem **too complex** for her now and*
   *leave her feeling anxious or ashamed of her own*
   *inability.*

This chapter includes selected fun activities designed to keep up with changes in an elder's interests and abilities. Your participation level as a visitor will increase, change and decrease as her health changes. The less mom remembers and can do, the more you will have to do or learn to do differently.

Other factors to consider include her personality, emotional and physical health, family history, and surprisingly to many people–gender. Male and female elders with Alzheimer's are very different. Unfortunately, I found that many of the activities available for elders with Alzheimer's disease were *gender-blended* to make it easier to instruct groups of people. These popular activities rarely address the very distinct differences that endure, despite memory loss, between men and women.

Many of the activities I found made every effort to include different backgrounds, religious interests, musical tastes and reading topics, *but this created another concern.* Few of us actually reflect America's mythical mainstream "melting pot." We are all different–especially in the things closest to our hearts. Most of us grew up with special ethnic, racial, educational, religious and family-specific rituals and beliefs–these are the things that may need refreshing. Each of these areas of life give us additional ways to validate the lives of our elders.

I found only a few activities or materials already available that fit Mom's interests and ability level *and* are appropriate for just the two of us. So, I created a new book, called a *Treasure Book*. It is especially designed to provide fun for Grace that is focused on her and engages both of us. I take *her Book* with me each time I visit although every visit may not leave time or energy to enjoy even one page. Mom beams whenever she sees the cover of *"her"* book because she knows, *"Something good is in it for me."*

Mom's *Book* has only ten pages and each one requires some up-front work on my part (about 20 minutes per page), some customizing time with Mom or a combination. Once each page is tailored just for her it can be read, looked at and enjoyed over and over for years to come, even if and when Mom can't talk This is where I put as much of *Grace* as I can possibly capture on the pages of a book. It is for both of us.

If your mom can see you and/or hear the sound of your voice, these brief but important pages will help both of you when you visit. This book also has another purpose. Because each page highlights a different aspect of mom's personality and her life, her participation in developing it and your shared experiences going though each activity will make it an enduring family treasure. This chapter gives examples of creative ways to entertain mom using *"her"* book. *(See Appendix for ordering information)*

## *Family Involvement*

Involving other family members in creating pages for mom's *Treasure Book* is a great idea. In some families, each member develops their own *Treasure Book* and shares it with mom when they visit. Each page becomes a unique story-collage arranged so that it:

> **Focuses on mom** *and highlights her life, her good times, adventures, talents and achievements in relation to others.*
>
> **Shows** *several different but related photos, pictures and clippings.*
>
> **Stimulates** *her senses with a variety of formats, colors, textures and shapes.*
>
> **Is easy to read** *with plain large type or hand printing instead of writing or fancy lettering.*

Another important difference in developing mom's book is
that it relies on you and your family's individual and
combined knowledge of her life–instead of questioning or
interviewing her about things and times she may no longer be
able to remember.

*Preparation Tips for*
## Mom's Treasure Book

**Colored background papers** acid-free or light
weight fabric from magazines, calendars, greeting
cards, favorite clothes, etc. One color should cover at
least 2/3 of the page to help mom recognize it.
Create a separate page for each topic.

**A photo of mom on each page** when she is happy,
perhaps an old school photo or some other occasion.
Her face in the photo should be no smaller than a
quarter. One or two photos or pictures of other
people or objects may be added–make sure they are
about quarter-size also. **DO NOT CROWD** the
page!

**Add a brief note**–block-printed or a short typed
excerpt from one or more of her favorite books,
poems, songs, etc. on white paper to the collage.
Add some humor on every page.

Each page should be interesting and attractive looking, but
not crowded. Each photo, picture, color or item on the page
should generate its own short story for you to relate to mom.
If mom can help put these pages together, so much the better.
This is not a lot of work, but it does require *creative* energy that
many visitors don't have or have in short supply. If you would

like this experience but don't have the time and/or energy to create your own book, use the pre-designed formats in the *Treasure Book*, or ask young people in your family to help.

When I see Grace, I ask her, *"Do you want to read from your book today?"* After a few visits, she decided on several "favorite" pages with activities she enjoys so we return to them many, many times. When the day comes and she can't remember what she likes, I will already know her favorites and I can talk about them and read to her. Selected topics and examples for this book are described on the following pages. Enjoy!

## 1. Reading Mom's Favorite Stories

I resisted reading *to* Grace for quite a while. I had great trouble admitting that she needed me to read to her. This was another one of the times when I could not escape the knowledge that she had a disease that would only get worse. One day while she was still at home with me, I noticed that she no longer even looked at the newspaper, her favorite women's magazines, *Family Circle* and *Woman's Day,* or even her beloved collection of recipes.

I knew she liked to read so I started reading *with* her. I helped her when she stumbled on difficult words or words that had become unfamiliar to her. Grace is embarrassed when she mispronounces words that she knows she has been able to read in the past. Now I read very short stories *to* her. This way she hears my voice while concentrating on and enjoying the story. We usually read sitting side-by-side, with her to my right, so she can easily see any pictures and maybe recognize a word or two here and there. When I read a short story, inspirational message or a brief news item I see a peaceful look in her eyes. I created a unique and helpful *elder reading-level* for use with aging adults. I use:

> *Short sentences of no more than ten (10) words each.*
> *One and two-syllable words as much as possible.*

This reading level is different from juvenile reading materials because it uses *mature topics* to reflect the elder's childhood years as well as their adult memories and experiences. Using these two key points as a guide, I can easily revise as I read material that may be too difficult for her to understand. My words have to be carefully chosen and adjusted for her changing needs.

### Guide: Reading Mom's Favorite Stories

This page is for the written word: short stories, inspirational or religious verses, newspaper articles, photos, awards etc. Starting with the page preparation tips, I printed the titles of five books, movies and television shows that were Grace's favorites over the years.

Each title creates its own short tale about a good time in her life. A newspaper headline (reduced in size) of an event she lived through can trigger good memories or a good story about her and what she did or where she was at that time.

I use the present tense when I read to Grace as much as possible and remind myself not to ask her, "Do you remember?"

## 2. Laughing Together

I've mentioned that some form of humor should be part of every page. This calls for some thought because mom's sense of humor may have changed considerably or seem to have disappeared altogether.

### Guide: Mom's Laughing Page

Using the collage tips, the "humor" page I created for Grace is filled with seven photos of her and other family members. Each photo we selected together because of the **hilarious hair-dos** everyone had over the years.

As soon as we turn to this page, she starts laughing–every time! We can talk about the people, herself included, their crazy hair styles, rate the beauticians we've known, do-it-ourself experiments, the events related to the hair concoction, how much it cost to look like that, etc.

Sharing the same page, each family member will have additional contributions and comments to make, but from their perspective. This is the page for jokes, funny poems, humorous stories, cartoons, photos, pictures and anything else that rates a chuckle from her.

## 3. Music: Singing, Playing & Listening

I thought I understood how important music was in setting, creating or changing our moods and emotions, but I really discovered how sounds and rhythms affect us during my travels around town with Grace a few years ago. . .

## Driving Me Crazy!

*A few years ago I began to dread being in the car with Grace. Our trips all started with joyful anticipation of a day of shopping or dining, but suddenly on the return trip her mood would change to gloom and doom. She became agitated about who-knows-what and the rest of our trip would be pure misery for both of us. Mom refused any plea to tell me what was wrong. Through puffed cheeks and gritted teeth, she would say, "You know what's wrong!" But I didn't have a clue and telling her that only made her angrier.*

*Somehow, I thought to change the music in the car from the usual jazz to something soothing that she might like. I tried several different types of music before I hit pay dirt! I discovered that she responds enthusiastically to male singers with deep, smooth voices. I immediately bought all the cassettes I could find in this category. Tony Bennett is her favorite, he has saved our lives.*

*Ever since this blessed discovery five years ago, I play one of these cassettes every time we go someplace. I also play them in the background during most visits. Mom never tires of hearing this music and often sings along with it. Miraculously she is calm, relaxed and in a good mood anytime "her" music is playing.*

If possible make opportunities for your mom to enjoy music during your visits. Author, Carmel Sheridan found, *"Listening to music can help a person with Alzheimer's to reach thoughts and feelings more easily."*

Some of her helpful suggestions are included below:

> **Geographic names** in songs and music like: "Chicago, Chicago," "Tennessee Waltz," and "I Left My Heart in San Francisco," etc.
>
> **Making music** is something many men and women with Alzheimer's still can enjoy. Elders often retain their ability to play musical instruments or sing. Using rhythm instruments like tambourines, shakers or a small drum can be very enjoyable because of the sounds and rhythms they make.
>
> **Personal names** in songs and music are engaging, such as: "Rambling Rose," "Goodnight, Irene," or "Danny Boy."
>
> **Big band music** is always a favorite with elders: Duke Ellington, Tommy Dorsey, Count Basie and Benny Goodman are ideal for triggering pleasant memories and special moments from the past.
>
> **Old-time radio shows** on cassettes are enjoyed, though usually for short periods of time, because of the familiar sounds and old-fashioned humor.
>
> **Marches, polkas and country tunes** with a strong beat are fun and popular.

On a recent visit I arrived in time to see Mom joyfully singing songs led by a local minister. I was quite surprised to discover how much she seemed to enjoy herself because I only had vague, long ago memories of her singing. I had an image of myself at about seven or eight years old, standing close by her as she taught me one of her songs and washed dishes. I loved trying to sing with her and marveled that she knew such beautiful music. I think she told me that her mother sang these songs with her when she was a little girl.

One day recently, the nursing home staff told me Grace joyfully participates whenever there is music or singing involved. I saw that she couldn't remember many of the words, but the expression on her face told me that the melodies brought back pleasant memories. She tried her best to sing every song. This day I learned that one of her favorite songs is *"Amazing Grace."* I didn't even know she knew it! Now we sing this song together often. The words touch me deeply every time, even as we struggle to stay in tune.

Nancy Mace, author of *The 36-Hour Day*, rates sing-a-longs as the most popular activity for people with memory loss.


## Guide: Mom's Music Page

A photo of mom singing, dancing, playing or enjoying music will spark a surprisingly joyful response. Use the collage tips to create a colorful musical masterpiece for this page. I include a handwritten list of her Top Ten Favorite Songs. It always triggers pleasant memories. I also put the pictures of three of her favorite musicians in a grouping.

I typed out two verses of "Amazing Grace" so both of us could remember the words. I bring a cassette with some of her favorites and we can listen or sing along as we visit. This is a beautiful and fun page.

## 4. Storytelling

Telling, reading and creating stories for Grace is probably the most enjoyable activity for both of us. I wrote my first story about her early youth using the *elder* reading level (p. 115) so she could read most of it herself. She could read and comprehend most of it with only a little help from me–that was a year ago. Today, she can only pick out one or two words here and there so I read the entire story to her. She enjoys hearing *"her"* story over and over; after all, she is its star.

Guide: Mom's Storytelling Page

On this page I pasted a story I wrote about Grace. I printed it in larger type so she would not have to strain to read it. The entire story is less than 500 words, uses short sentences and has only a few "big" words. I used a photo of her graduating from college. Here is a very brief excerpt:

### *Little Grace Gets Her Wish*

Once upon a time there was a beautiful little girl named Grace. She was an only child, but she always wanted a brother or a sister, especially a sister. But her beloved mother died suddenly when she was only seventeen years old. She went to college where she met and later married a handsome, young man. . .

Many years went by before she got pregnant again. With tears in her eyes, she called her third child, Kay which was like her own mother's name, Katie. *The End*

Don't worry about grammar, just write her story the way you talk.

## 5. Celebrating

Celebrating holidays or other special occasions will never be as they used to be, but we can still have fun and enjoy ourselves. One tricky part of celebrations is trying to figure out what to give someone who has Alzheimer's. Grace's actual need for "presents" is minimal and I had to change my own traditional ideas of what to give her and what to do when celebrating special times. The best gifts for Mom now are whatever gives her joy in the moment they are given.

I found some fresh ideas in the *Baby Boomers Guide to Caring for Aging Parents.* The author, Bart Astor, clarifies several puzzling issues related to Mom's care and gifts that fit her current needs and living situation, including:

*Clothes: Housecoats, lightweight long-sleeved shirt jackets, socks, comfortable shoes that are easy to put on, pajamas, etc. Make sure everything has pockets!*

*Personal Items: Grooming items like toothpaste, lipstick, tissues, hand lotion, etc.*

*Entertainment Items: Letters from friends or relatives, family photos, junk mail to open, music cassettes, greeting cards, etc.*

*Room Decorations: Extra blanket, comforter, personalized wall calendar, silk flowers and stuffed toys.*

Sometimes I bring Grace a gift-wrapped, brightly-colored T-shirt. She is as delighted as some people would be if it were a diamond ring. The pleasure, however, lasts for less than 30 seconds–there is only so much I can say about a T-shirt.

As soon as we put it down, she forgets about it. If she sees the shirt on the bed before I put it in the closet, she has another burst of surprise and delight. It is important for us to make sure she has the *"things"* she likes and needs, but we have to adjust our ideas about the traditional importance of presents. What she appreciates now is the caring time and attention she gets from the staff and from people she still recognizes.

I ignored the advice of one caregiver who suggested that I get clothes for Mom from thrift shops or garage sales because *"she won't know the difference."* But I know. Mom has always taken care to be neat and stylish–I think she would like to continue looking that way. I make sure she has the kind of clothes I think she would pick out for herself: warm, bright colors, well-fitted, coordinated, and most of all, stylish. Whenever she has a moment of clarity and looks at her clothes or sees her reflection in a mirror, I want her to see familiar clothes that *"look nice"*on her.

## Creating Our Own Celebrations

When Grace's first birthday, first Mother's Day, first Thanksgiving, and the big one–the first Christmas–in the nursing home came, we faced major creative challenges and opportunities. Celebrating these *first times* during the year meant doing new and unfamiliar things for both of us. At first, these occasions were emotionally difficult for me, but monumentally more difficult for Mom. She doesn't know when her birthday is or any other day for that matter.

On her first birthday in the nursing home, I took her to the best restaurant in town. I had a small birthday cake with a lighted candle delivered to our table. She enjoyed the excitement it created, but seemed slightly confused about blowing out the candle and making a wish. She and I slowly read the birthday cards from my brother, sister and myself. She loved hearing the beautiful words about her and how wonderful we feel she is to us. Grace enjoyed the food and vaguely knew we were in a special place. We enjoyed being together and this was as much as could happen.

Creating new traditions did not come easily for me. As our first Thanksgiving approached, I was filled with loving, happy memories and painful emotions and regrets. Then I decided to become an *artist of celebration.* I had no idea what was going to happen, but I just *trusted* that it would work out. . .

### Room in the Inn

*I did not have a celebration plan. What I wanted was a small restaurant with a "home-like" atmosphere that served food Grace would like. Although I started weeks early, every place I called for reservations was filled. No new ideas occurred to me even as I drove to pick her up on that sunny Thanksgiving morning. The only place available was a Howard Johnson-like restaurant in Flagstaff–so off we went.*

*As we drove on the winding mountain road, I told her that this was Thanksgiving Day. I said, "I'm most thankful for your good health, but most of all because you are such a good mom." Then I asked her, "What about you Mom, what are you most thankful for today?" She thought for a second before a sweet smile crossed her face. "You," she said. I exhaled deeply. I just had to find a suitable place.*

*Our chances of finding a great place on Thanksgiving day dwindled by the minute. Suddenly we spotted a small inn where we had enjoyed many great breakfasts in the summer months. It seemed unlikely that such a place would be available, but I had to try anyway. We pulled into the sparsely filled parking lot of the Junipine Lodge–this did not look good. It was ten minutes to twelve.*

*The only person I saw was a young woman, she was sweeping the front porch. I timidly called out to her, "Are you serving dinner today?" To my great surprise, she said, "Yes, we are, we'll be open in ten minutes." She hesitated before saying, "But all we have left is one table, it's for two. How many are in your party?"*

*If I had planned the day, it could not have turned out better. The restaurant seats only 25 friendly diners, the traditional family-style meal was delicious–they had everything Grace loved to eat. I had never been so thankful.*

## Guide: Mom's Celebration Page

This page was one of the easiest to make because there are many photos and reminders of family celebrations. I used the collage tips to create the background. The photos of our family and friends eating the fabulous meals Grace cooked bring back many stories of good times, good food and good people. I included a list of five holidays to trigger additional comments and stories. A photo of Mom opening a present and the expression on her face brings her joy each time she sees it.

Chapter 7:

# Ten Visiting Guides

*One kind of visit does not fit all situations.* There are several variables involved, like how your mom is doing that day, your intent, what you do. Even the time of day or the weather can have a definite impact on your visit. This chapter describes ten types of visits for various situations and relationships. All visits maintain some form of the Eight Great Habits discussed in Chapter Five, however, each visit has its own timeframe and purpose.

### Ten Visiting Guides

| | | |
|---|---|---|
| #1 Maxi-Visits | #6 | Celebration Visits |
| #2 Out and About Visits | #7 | Care Conferences |
| #3 Long-Distance Visits | #8 | Occasional Visit(s) |
| #4 Family Visits | #9 | Emergency Visits |
| #5 Create-A-Visit | #10 | Micro-Visits |

Having a set of reasonable guides for visiting Mom relieves some of the pressure I felt about whether or not I was doing all I could. I began by memorizing the *Eight Great Habits* and mentally checked them off during our visits until I established a comfortable pattern. Now I rarely think about them, they are a natural part of what I do each time.

As time goes by, my visiting role and responsibilities change and increase while Mom's ability to communicate slowly and sometimes dramatically declines. Changing our communication patterns greatly impacts our time together because:

1. *She may not speak because she has lost all or most of that ability.*
2. *She may not desire to talk or respond to you or anyone at that moment.*
3. *Her attention span may be short or at best, she may seem unfocused and not pay much attention to you.*
4. *She may not seem to recognize you or think you are someone else.*
5. *Mom may speak, but all you hear is "gibberish."*
6. *She may be verbally abusive or physically combative.*

If one or more of these or other situations occurs when you visit, it is sure to make an already complex time more difficult. However, it doesn't have to be the end of your visits. It may mean that it's time to change to another type of visit like the **Micro-Visit**. The following *Guides* suggest activity timelines that fit changing circumstances. The suggested times show that visits don't have to take all day to have a positive outcome, but *preparation* and knowing your *options* is what makes for the best possible visit, every time.

# #1 - The Maxi-Visit

The Maxi Visit is the kind of visit I have most of the time I see Grace. This is one of the most intensive and emotionally involving visits and it is not for everyone. Nor does it work well for every visit. My usual visit lasts from 90 minutes to three hours and I see Grace two or three times each week. This works well for both of us at this time.

| Time | Habits | #1 MAXI-Visits |
|---|---|---|
| 5 | Preparation | Bring Visiting Bag |
| 5 | Information | Check health/issues with staff |
| 5 | Greeting | Greet mom, give "treats" |
| 10 | Attention | Examine room, clothes, grooming, |
| 15 | Communication | Talk, listen, encourage response |
| 20 | Arts/Crafts | Read, play music, sing, tell stories, |
| 15 | Activity | Short walk, grooming, eat, toilet |
| 5 | Reassurance | Say goodbye to mom, staff |

*80 minutes minimum time*

What does not work well is *breaking the pattern*, as I found out recently. Grace knows that whenever I visit it means we will take a walk, no matter how short. Once I just popped in for a *Micro-Visit* of about 30 minutes and we did not have time for our usual walk. Unlike other visits she became slightly agitated at the change in our routine. Since then, I make sure I have time for a *real* visit and spend one or more hours with her. My intent is to make sure Mom does not feel abandoned and that she knows she is being cared for and loved. I find that regular visits two or three times every week are manage-able for me and seem to come at a comfortable interval for her. This schedule of visits leaves me slightly tired, but not overwhelmed. I make sure I plan my visits so I have plenty of time and don't feel or appear rushed. She needs my full attention.

I take two **Visiting Bags**, a large one with all the things I think I'll need for Mom, and a smaller one with treats for her to carry. She likes to carry bags, I think it reminds her of her purse. Mom's bag usually has a piece of fresh fruit (bananas and apples create less mess) a cookie, muffin or a tiny box of raisins, and a small book or colorful greeting card to read.

The *Maxi-Visit* is not for everyone. It is most appropriate for close family and friends because of the intense involvement needed and the intimate attention given to every aspect of mom's care, including feeding and toileting.

# #2 - Out And About Visits

*Out & About Visits* can be a blessing or a curse. Going out depends on Mom's needs and desires as well as my energy level. Grace is continent so we manage well with one or two toilet breaks. (*I don't recommend going out for moms who are incontinent.*) I always make sure we use the toilet before *and* after each of our outings. We go to one of three local restaurants for lunch once or twice a week. Afterwards, we sometimes stop at a nearby ice cream parlor for dessert. Mom enjoys riding in the car so where we go doesn't matter to her.

| Time | Habits | #2 OUT AND ABOUT Visits |
|---|---|---|
| 5 | Preparation | Bring Visiting Bag |
| 5 | Information | Check health/issues with staff |
| 5 | Greeting | Greet mom, give "treats", ask *if* she would like to go out today |
| 5 | Attention | Examine room, clothes, grooming, |
| 10 | Communication | Talk, listen, encourage response |
| 15 | Arts/Crafts, | Read, play music, sing, tell stories |
| 60 | Activity | Restaurant, art fair, shopping, walk, garden, toilet, etc. |
| 15 | Reassurance | Say goodbye to mom, help her get settled in her room |

*2 hours minimum time*

Another concern for outings is to make sure Mom gets plenty of rest breaks–places where we sit in the shade and chat or just rest quietly. Sometimes we are out for four or five hours.

## Visiting Mom

This happens when we drive down to Phoenix for a special lunch and a little window-shopping. She really enjoys these trips, they are so like what we have always done. Of course, I play *her* music the entire time we are in the car. These longer trips have worked out well so far, but I look for any signs that this type of trip may not be suitable for her anymore. I think I will know—when Mom and I are *not* having fun and decide that it takes too much effort to go outside the home.

If you are taking your mom to places by car, you will need to carry *emergency equipment* on each trip. You will need: a flashlight; small first aid kit; blanket; tissue; drinking water; and if at all possible, a cell phone. As time goes on traveling in the car may become impractical. When and if this happens, we will spend more time enjoying the patio area at the nursing home.

# #3 - Long-Distance Visits

Many people do not live close by their mom and must travel considerable distances to see her, so, their visits may be less frequent and may be shorter. If you are in this situation and you are mom's primary or only caregiver, you want to make sure to have the best visit possible, in addition to handling the *business* end of mom's care. Sometimes you may need to spend time with mom and then have a *Care Conference*. These are both weighty responsibilities, so efficient planning is important to long-distance visitors.

| Time | Habits | #3 LONG-DISTANCE Visits |
|------|--------|--------------------------|
| 5 | Preparation | Bring Visiting Bag |
| 10 | Information | Check with staff, aides, residents |
| 10 | Greeting | Greet mom, re-introduce yourself, give "treats" |
| 10 | Attention | Examine room, clothes, grooming, |
| 10 | Communication | Talk, listen, encourage response |
| 15 | Arts/Crafts | Read, sing, play music, tell stories |
| 10 | Activity | Massage, walk, grooming toilet |
| 10 | Reassurance | Say goodbye to mom |

*80 minutes minimum time*

Long-distance visitors have to intensify what they do in *every* part of their visit. Use all your senses to discover everything that is different, better or worse, from your previous visit. Start *gathering information* the second you open the door where mom lives. You are looking to see if things seem to be running smoothly. Don't ignore your intuition if you feel that *"something's not right here."* Is the place clean, orderly, well-lighted, etc. How do the residents look? Is there a sustained odor?

Stop at the nurses' station or speak with the caregiver to ask about mom *before* going to see her. Call ahead to make sure someone will be available for a brief update when you arrive. If you haven't seen mom in over a week, prepare to find mild to dramatic physical and/or emotional changes. Mom's changes can be startling, but you can prepare for them better if you *expect* to find differences.

### My, How You've Changed

*Robin knew to prepare herself for changes when she flew across country to see her beloved grandmother. But the reality of seeing her change was still dramatically surprising. She recalls feeling a sharp, cold blast as soon as she saw her grandmother.*

*"Gram wasn't dressed right," she told me with a far-away look in her eyes. "She has always been so stylish and always coordinated everything she wore. . . this time. . . she was wearing strange-looking clothes."*

*"We've always had such lively talks, but this time there were these 'silences'. . . Only a year ago she was in a bowling league, but now she is sort of tentative in her movements. She used to always have an envelope full of photos of her grandchildren to show off to her friends, but. . .not now."*

It helps a lot for us to anticipate change, as long as we know that no amount of mental preparation will completely steady our hearts when we see mom after an absence of months, weeks or even a few days. Mom may look, speak and act differently and she may not remember you. Gently *re-intro-duce* yourself. The warmth of your greeting takes on new importance. Go to her room. Give mom her "treat" and sit down together. Check the room out completely, visually and by opening and closing doors. How is mom dressed and groomed? How does she *really* look and sound to you?

Your visit can be very exciting to mom, so calming words and activities may be very appropriate. Listening to favorite music in the background is a good start, it can be the same every time. Taking mom to the toilet is important. Try to establish a kind of *pattern* to your visits.

Touching mom is one of the most caring things you can do when you don't see her often, but not everyone likes or wants to be touched. Ask her first if it's O.K. to touch or hold her. Helping to groom her hair and nails is one way to make this happen. I found that giving Grace a pedicure and rubbing lotion on her feet and lower legs is very relaxing to her.

Use tips given in previous chapters to make each long-distance visit the best possible. The time guides for this type of visit depend entirely on mom's health and her needs. Just before you leave, sit down and take your time saying goodbye to her.

# #4 - Family Visits

A family visit means two or more family members or close friends are in the same room with mom.  A good rule of thumb for family visits is to keep the gathering as small as possible.  It's too easy to get mom confused or anxious when several people are giving her attention and expecting her to respond.  Mom may have trouble on some of her best days just remembering who she is, so expecting her to remember and socialize with a roomful of relatives may be asking too much. You and your family will have to decide what is best for her.  Be gentle.

| Time | Habits | #4  FAMILY Visits |
|---|---|---|
| 5 | Preparation | Bring Visiting Bag |
| 5 | Information | Check with staff, ask for a private room |
| 5 | Greeting | Greet mom and make introductions–one at a time, give "treats" |
| 5 | Attention | Examine room, clothes, grooming |
| 15 | Communication | Talk, listen, encourage response, avoid loud talking/music or sudden noises/movements |
| 10 | Arts/Crafts | Read, play music, tell stories, etc. |
| 10 | Activity | Short walk, grooming, toilet |
| 10 | Reassurance | Each person says goodbye to mom, help get her re-settled |

*65  minutes minimum time*

Kids of any age are always welcome visitors, especially when they understand how important it is to move slowly and speak softly–no running, skipping or loud talking. A family visit can be the highlight of everyone's week. One way to bring this about is to make sure each family member understands as much as possible about Alzheimer's disease, how it is affecting mom and what they can expect in mom's new environment. With this background, it will be easier to keep the focus of your visit on mom and her needs. If everyone has some preparation ahead of time, it won't upset their apple cart completely if mom gets anxious when she sees a group of people *(her family)* but wants to return to the activity room–to be with her friends.

Allow extra time at the end of a family visit for one or two family members to help mom get calmly resettled back in her room or with other residents.

# #5 - Create-A-Visit

Creating-A-Visit can be fun for both you and mom. The success of this type of visit depends on your creativity and the amount of time and effort you invest to prepare for a unique occasion. These visits include features from other types of visits combined with your own creativity and mom's needs. *Create-A-Visits* are sometimes the easiest kind of visit to put together because they meet our individual needs. It is usually a good idea to experience several other types of visits *before* advancing to this freer form.

| Time | Habits | #5 CREATE-A-VISIT |
|---|---|---|
| 5 | Preparation | Bring Visiting Bag |
| 5 | Information | Check with staff and aides |
| 5 | Greeting | Greet mom, give "treats" |
| 5 | Attention | Visually check room, clothes, etc. |

*(The next three visiting habits–communication, arts and crafts, and physical activity–can be combined, omitted, or expanded as needed.)*

| Time | Habits | |
|---|---|---|
| 10 | Communication | Talk, listen, encourage response |
| 10 | Arts/Crafts | Read, listen to music, tell stories |
| 10 | Activity | Short walk, grooming and/or toilet |
| 5 | Reassurance | Say goodbye to mom |

*55 minutes minimum time*

Every component of the visit is up for change–how you do that is your choice. Keep in mind that the shorter the visit, the more experience you need in order to cover everything that needs to be done in an effective way.

Grace and I spontaneously created this type of visit. First I wanted to be sure this was a good day to have a special activity. When I arrived, I found that she was calm and open for a slightly different activity. Because I had last seen her only three days ago, I did not have to spend a lot of time attending to many of my usual "housekeeping" duties such as checking the clean clothes supply, room cleanliness, medication schedule, etc.

I wanted to engage her in developing pages for her **Treasure Book.** I planned for us to sit in the patio area selecting family pictures to put in it. I brought *copies* of photos that were already the right size (head shots at least the size of a quarter) for her book. We talked about each picture (several times). I told her short stories about each person and what I knew about their place in her life. Many of the pictures brought instant smiles as Grace recognized friendly, loving faces from her past. Sometimes she was delighted just to remember their names! We spent over an hour telling stories, laughing, selecting photos, cutting, pasting and finally, arranging them on the pages of her book. We did not need music this time because the birds and the other natural sights and sounds of the outdoors provided a stimulating environment in which to be creative.

# #6 - Celebration Visits

Of the ten types of visits, this one demands the most creativity on your part and the most sensitivity about mom's abilities and needs. *Celebration Visits* and *Family Visits* are very similar, but there are some differences. A major difference is that *celebrations* can be held with only one visitor as well as with a group of visitors. Grace and I have celebrations with just the two of us on many special occasions and holidays because my brother and sister live farther away.

| Time | Habits | **#6 CELEBRATION Visits** |
|------|--------|---------------------------|
| 5 | Preparation | Bring Visiting Bag |
| 5 | Information | Check with staff and aides |
| 10 | Greeting | Greet mom, tell her your plans for a special celebration–different activity, new/more people, travel |
| 5 | Attention | Examine room, clothes, grooming |

*(The next three activities can be combined in any way to suit the type of celebration, mom's needs and her ability to participate.)*

| Time | Habits | |
|------|--------|---|
| 15 | Communication | Talk, listen, give treats,presents |
| 15 | Arts/Crafts | Read, music, tell stories, etc. |
| 15 | Physical Activity | Short walk, grooming and/or toilet |
| 5 | Reassurance | Say goodbye to mom |

*75 minutes minimum time*

Celebrations can also be a mixed blessing because for each occasion, we will probably have to *create new ways* to celebrate so that mom enjoys the day too. Creativity plays a big part because it means taking the best from our *traditional* celebrations and meshing it with what works well for mom today.

My mother is delighted when I tell her we are celebrating her birthday, but two minutes later, I find she has completely forgotten her birthday or our celebration. Blowing out the candles and making a wish are forgotten traditions. Grace was able to join in when I changed the focus to *a celebration just for you.* She liked singing *Happy Birthday,* but the fact that it was *her* birthday and the meaning of "birthday" were both lost. However, she joyfully opened the gift-wrapped present and said, *"It's sooo pretty, thank you very much."* Her present was a new (inexpensive) watch to replace the one she recently lost. Grace can't tell time anymore, she even has trouble telling one day from the next, but she always knows *if* her watch is missing from her wrist. Everyone around her knows too because she tells them.

All of the tips about crowds mentioned in *Family Visits* apply to celebrations. If giving mom a present is appropriate, wrap it in colorful paper with a ribbon that comes off easily. Don't be surprised if she is more excited about the wrapping than about the present. If you have trouble thinking of a suitable gift for her, review the gift list given in *Chapter 6 (p. 121).*

# #7 - Care Conferences

This is the only visit that may not involve seeing mom. Instead, you will meet with one or more staff to formally discuss how mom is doing, her health issues, activities, etc. Do not settle for vague reports like, *"Your mom is just the same, there's no change."* Everything in the universe changes all the time, mom is no exception. This broad comment could mask neglect or worse. It would be a good idea to follow the advice Grace frequently gave us–*Question everything!*

| Time | Habits | #7 CARE CONFERENCES |
|---|---|---|
| 10 | Preparation | Prepare a "checklist" of questions you want answered about mom and her care |
| 5 | Information | Briefly check with nurse about mom's current health situation, etc., locate private meeting place for care conference |
| 15 | Communication | **LISTEN,** talk, **ASK** questions, comment, complain, compliment |
| 10 | Parting | Confirm any of your prior requests for care. Sign-off only *after* carefully reading mom's care sheet. Say goodbye to staff, make next care conference appointment. |

*40 minutes minimum time*

I must have inherited my own questioning attitude from Grace. Even now, with Alzheimer's breaking down the door to her memory, she still practices what she so often preached to us long ago.

A few years back, her doctor told me to take Grace to the hospital emergency room to see about a mysteriously throbbing vein in her neck . . .

### "Don't YOU Know?"

*"She's wacked out," the doctor whispered to the incoming quartet of stone-faced specialists. They brushed past him and entered the hospital examination room where Mom and I waited. As if on cue, they arranged themselves in a tight semi-circle and stood completely still in front of her. No one spoke, but all eyes were on her.*

*The lead specialist produced a tiny flashlight and shone it in her eyes. It wasn't clear what he had seen, but after a minute he gave up with the light and stepped back. Finally, he broke the silence speaking for the first time. "Do you know where we are?" he asked in a bland voice. Mom's eyes widened. "Don't YOU know?" she demanded. When he spoke again, he raised his voice slightly. "Do YOU know where YOU are?" Mom had one eyebrow cocked when she responded. "Yes, I'm right here!" as she impatiently jabbed her index finger at the examining table beneath her.*

*The specialist roused himself once more. "Do you know what place this is?" All heads swiveled expectantly towards Grace–waiting. She looked him over from head to toe before she hissed, "This is the place where people come who have trouble,*

*They come here to get fixed!"*
*Then, she leaned toward me and in a whisper meant for*
*all to hear, she firmly said: "I do not want him operating*
*on me. He doesn't KNOW anything!"*

When we were growing up, Grace frequently told us to *"think for yourself!"* Even Alzheimer's disease could not take this lesson from her. This experience made me very aware of the importance of the attitudes of medical professionals toward elders, and their understanding or lack of knowledge about their conditions. Her response to them will often influence and determine their diagnosis and eventual treatment. We are responsible for knowing enough about mom to help the doctor *by giving our input.*

Last week as I talked with an aide before leaving Grace, a visitor marched into the nurses' station, interrupted us and began questioning the aide. . .

*"Do you prescribe my husband's medications?" she softly*
*demanded, but she was shaking with barely restrained*
*emotion." The aide tensed up and quickly denied any*
*knowledge or ability to give medicines. He directed*
*her to the nurse.*
*"He doesn't seem like himself," she continued. He's*
*sleeping all day and night! Maybe he's getting too much*
*medicine? What medicine is he getting?"*

I found out later that she had spent several sleepless nights worrying about the changes she saw in her husband, but had said nothing about it because, *"I'm not one to make waves."* I think Grace would gently encourage her to: *Speak up!*

Many care facilities have a regular six-month schedule for these conferences. However, in Grace's first eight months, I requested three additional conferences. I probably will not ask for as many meetings in the future, but I started out this way so I could learn about and monitor Mom's new environment. As caregivers and family we are *not* at the mercy of staff schedules–we can and must speak up and request a conference whenever we want more detailed information about our elders.

The staff has an official process they follow which covers many different areas of Grace's day-to-day care and activities, including: medication schedules, tolerance and reaction; eating habits and diet adjustments; activity likes/dislikes and her participation levels; descriptions of any outbursts or acts of aggression; and toileting habits and concerns. I found these meetings with the administrator, social worker, nurse and sometimes an aide to be very informative. They increase my understanding about how she lives now. We are now "advocates."

As thorough as these sessions seem, I *always* have additional questions of my own. My questions are about: the bathing process; why it takes two to three weeks to get laundry back; who watches the hallways at night; how often the rooms are cleaned; why recent staff changes occurred; etc. I did not want to forget my concerns between care conferences, so I made up a **Care Sheet**. I look for any changes in:

| | |
|---|---|
| 1. *Room* | 7. *Activities* |
| 2. *Food* | 8. *Hygiene* |
| 3. *Medical staff* | 9. *Exercise* |
| 4. *Sleep* | 10. *Toilet* |
| 5. *Relationships* | 11. *Health* |
| 6. *Bathing* | 12. *Grooming* |

I go over this list *before* my conference and make brief notes. *After* staff gives me their report, I bring up any item not covered to my satisfaction. This is a good time to get a complete update of all medications, dosages and effects. Make sure you know everything and are comfortable with the kind and amount of medicines mom receives. If you are not, do not sign your agreement. You can always,"Just say *no.*" Get a second medical opinion. Always question *authority.*

Cathy, the new administrator in Grace's unit, is proactive and plain-spoken. Once when I asked for something special for Grace, she assured me she would look at what is best for everyone and see how she could make arrangements for Mom. I liked her approach because it told me that she is looking out for everyone and no one is left out.

Before the conference ends, be sure to compliment the staff on the things you are most pleased about regarding Mom's care. Saying, *"Thanks"* or *"Good Job"* is not clear enough. Instead, be specific: *"Please tell Sara we appreciate how quickly she noticed mom's flu symptoms–she was able to recover in just a few days,"* or *"The John that the cleaning crew really keeps mom's room fresh and clean."* Be specific and genuine as you reinforce behaviors you want to see continued. Don't be surprised if the staff modestly responds with,*"Oh, we're just doing our job."* The pleased look on their faces will tell you just how much they like having their efforts acknowledged and appreciated.

*"Question everything!"*

# #8 - Occasional Visits

Occasional visits have the power to bring enormous joy to the elder and to the visitor. It ensures the best visit possible if you see the elder infrequently, or this may be the only time you visit. Usually relatives, friends, co-workers, neighbors, or religious/spiritual leaders take advantage of this kind of visit. You may be strangers, but your desire to bring comfort and caring attention is still important. I found a few guidelines to help make this time together as enjoyable and beneficial as possible for both of you.

| Time | Habits | #8 OCCASIONAL Visits |
|---|---|---|
| 5 | Preparation | *Bring Visiting Bag* |
| 5 | Information | *Check-in with staff, get update* |
| 5 | Greeting | *Greet elder, introduce yourself, give "treats," sit down at eye-level, touch hands if this is appropriate* |
| 5 | Attention | *Casually note surroundings, clothes, grooming, etc.* |
| 10 | Communication | *Talk, listen, encourage response* |
| 5 | Arts/Crafts | *Read, listen to music, tell stories* |
| 5 | Activity | *Short walk (hold arm for support)* |
| 5 | Reassurance | *Say goodbyes, check with staff* |
| 40 | *minutes minimum time* | |

If you haven't seen the elder for a while or you are not familiar with the effects of Alzheimer's disease, be prepared to find many changes. Sometimes there will be dramatic physical decline as well as new, unsettling behaviors. Some changes appear over a period of just a few days or weeks. Expect conversation to be limited and different from whatever you are used to, but not impossible. Keep in mind to move slowly, speak clearly using simple words and short sentences, and to look into her eyes as much possible. Allow silences to occur naturally. *Do not expect her to entertain you.*

You have the challenge and opportunity for a fresh approach to an old relationship. The time you spend now is for the elder you are visiting and you will benefit, too. She may appreciate your time and effort in her own way, but still want to return to her friends or the privacy of her room soon after you arrive. This may be upsetting, but do not let this discourage you altogether. Your good intentions, preparation, time, and effort to see her are what really count–she will know this.

# #9 - Emergency Visits

Hearing words like, "*Your mother had a fall, can you come right away?*" can cause major panic, but it doesn't necessarily mean you have to fall apart. It is possible to prepare for an emergency call like this and reduce some of the stress that normally occurs.

### "One Word"

*Grant recently got such a call. He immediately dropped what he was doing and drove straight to the hospital. Nursing home staff met him at the door and briefly filled him in on his mother's condition. He wanted to find out more and asked to speak to the hospital doctor assigned to his mother. However, he realized the only thing he wanted at that moment was to "see" his mother. So off he rushed to her room . . .*

*When Grant found her room he was relieved to find her sleeping quietly, but he flinched at the sight of the dried blood and stitches on her forehead. However, just being able to look at her and hear her soft breathing was tremendously calming. After a few moments he realized he had been too panicked to find out details about her condition.*

*Asking basic questions* like: who, what, when, where, how, and what now, is critical. So is *taking notes* on what the doctor says. This is especially important later when you try to recall what was said or accurately relay information to other family members.

> *After a while Grant's mom opened her eyes, he was sitting next to her bed. As he held her cool hand he quietly asked, "Are you feeling better, Mom?" She strained to focus on his face. When her eyes settled on his, he saw the faintest flicker of recognition. Then she weakly responded with a single raspy word, "Yes." He was astonished at the powerful rush of grateful emotions her one word brought to him. This was the first time she had spoken in the past five months! A few days later, Grant learned that this was her last word—and he had been there to hear it.*

| Time | Habits | #9  EMERGENCY Visits |
|------|--------|----------------------|
| 5 | Preparation | *Bring Visiting Bag* |
| 10 | Information | **ASK** *for info, take notes, talk to staff* |
| 5 | Greeting | *Greet mom, express concern/comfort* |
| 5 | Attention | *Look over room, clothes, grooming* |
| 10 | Communication | **Listen**, *talk, encourage response* |
| 10 | Arts/Crafts | **Silence**, *read, music, tell stories* |
| 10 | Activity | **Sit quietly**, *short walk, grooming* |
| 5 | Reassurance | *Say goodbye to mom, staff* |
| 60 | minutes minimum time | |

Being prepared in case of emergencies is easy to do. In addition to the *Visiting Bag* I keep in my car for regular visits, I keep a similar one at home for times like this. I don't need the extra pressure and frustration of trying to get personal items together if Grace has an emergency.

This *Emergency Visiting Bag* is a little different, it contains: a lightweight robe, slippers, a full change of clothes, and two small books (one for each of you).

Grant says that a cell phone should also be part of the *Emergency Visiting Bag...."Our cell phone was a big help during this emergency. It let me stay right there with Mom while my wife called family members and medical staff."* If you don't have a cell phone, it's important to have a phone card with you at all times that you can use at any telephone.

# #10 - The Micro-Visit

Every visitor needs to know how to have a *45-minute Micro-Visit*. It's not always possible or necessary to stay for hours and hours. Once the *Eight Great Habits* are covered, you can be confident that this brief visit may be the best visit possible at that time. However, *Micro-Visits* can be very unfulfilling for you and mom, if not done properly.

*Caution: Micro-Visits require visiting skill and experience.*

The minimum timeline suggested below gives an idea of the kind of differences involved in this shorter type of visit. Short, however, does not mean *rushed*. Take your time and complete each part with care.

| Time | Habits | #10  The MICRO-Visit |
|---|---|---|
| 5 | Preparation | Bring Visiting Bag |
| 5 | Information | Check with staff and aides |
| 5 | Greeting | Greet mom, give "treats" |
| 5 | Attention | Examine room, clothes, grooming |

*(Any or all of the next three activities may be changed or even omitted depending on the elder's desires, behaviors or health conditions)*

| | | |
|---|---|---|
| 5 | Communication | Talk, listen, encourage response |
| 10 | Arts/Crafts | Read, music, tell stories, etc. |
| 5 | Activity | Grooming and/or toilet |
| 5 | Reassurance | Say goodbye to mom |

*45  minutes minimum time*

The key differences between *Micros* and other visits is that they occur less frequently, less time is spent with mom and there is a different emphasis on the ways you spend your time when you are there.

Sometimes *Micro-Visits* are best for everyone. It is especially appropriate when you have a difficult time being with your mother or elder—for whatever reason. If, when you leave her, you routinely feel verbally or emotionally abused or hurt, visiting becomes very painful. Arguing with a person who has Alzheimer's is NOT an option. It may be time to try a *Micro* and give both of you a break.

As Alzheimer's disease progresses, it frequently becomes more difficult to communicate with mom and you may want to stop visiting altogether. I've heard some visitors reason that, *"Mom doesn't know whether I come or not."* That may or may not be true, but you know. I wouldn't be totally positive that mom does not know you are there. She may be aware at some level for just a brief moment, and that may be enough for her.

During the *Micro*, the SOUND of your voice and your TOUCH may become the primary means of communicating with her. If mom is barely conscious or sleeps most of the time, your ability to communicate with her through talking, singing, reading and/or storytelling are critical. You need experience practicing these visiting habits and activities.

Touching mom depends on permission from both of you. Some people don't like much or any touching. Be as sensitive to mom's needs and desires about this as possible. You may also have some ideas of touching that make this simple act an

issue. Previous chapters discuss ways to touch that communicate your caring thoughts and feelings. *Micros* can be even
shorter than the suggested minimum time because of mom's
health. Use the *Micro* whenever needed–trust your own
judgment. It will give you and mom *the best visit possible.*

## *Afterwords...*

There are still things I want to say, even after all these words. I am thankful I had a chance to write about my experience with Grace and share our journey with others. I revealed some of my inner conflicts, spiritual questions, doubts and fears that arose as I attempted to understand all that she was experiencing in her new private world. To me this means *she's gone ahead*–that's where she is now. She is safe and loved and at peace. I will walk this road with her for as long as I live, for as long as she needs me.

Throughout Grace's life she has read from *The Daily Word*, an inspirational book published monthly by Unity School. There are only about 150 words on each day's page–how perfect! Grace can't read much these days, a word or two here and there, but when I read to her she listens to every word. I see her quietly going inside herself as she hears me read the inspiration for the day. I read a page or two to her as a frequent part of many of our visits. When I finish reading a passage she always says, *"That's really true,"* or *"That's good,"* as she thoughtfully nods her head. I was slow in realizing that she might want and need help praying.

I am no longer filled with tears of fear. Finally, I am at peace within myself. I know in my heart that even as her Alzheimer's progresses, she is in a place where she is loved and cared for. I know also that we will always be together.

There are many types of books with daily thoughts in them suitable for inspirational reading–it's important that Grace hears words that touch her heart. I change many of the "big" words to ones that are easier for her to understand as I read aloud to her.

I know she is being cared for in ways that are beyond my understanding, I no longer *need* to know the details. I trust this is so because just at the moment that thought occurred I found myself reaching for one of her *Daily Word* books. There was a pile of twenty or so older issues on the table next to me. I randomly picked up one book and opened it. The page I casually turned to instantly brought me deep comfort. It began with this message:

Tuesday, October 13, 1998
*"I give thanks for grace . . ."*

# Appendix

## CHAPTER 1

Anderson, Beverly. *Useful Tips & Resources for a Caregiver,* Northern Arizona Chapter of the Alzheimer's Association, Prescott, AZ, 1999

Billing, Nathan. *To Be Old and Sad*–Understanding Depression in the Elderly, Lexington Books, Lexington, MA, 1987.

Sparks, Nicholas. *The Notebook: A Novel,* Warner Books, Inc., New York, NY, 1996.

Strauss, Peter J; and Lederman, Nancy M. *The Elder Law Handbook:* A Legal and Financial Survival Guide for Caregivers and Seniors, Facts On File, Inc. New York, NY, 1996.

## CHAPTER 2

Breathnach, Sarah Ban. *The Simple Abundance Journal of Gratitude,* A Time Warner Company, New York, NY, 1996.

Canfield, Jack et. al., *Chicken Soup for the Mother's Soul:* 101 Stories to Open the Hearts and Rekindle the Spirits of Mothers, Health Communications, Inc., Deerfield Beach, FL, 1997.

Gray-Davidson, Frena. *The Alzheimer's Sourcebook for Caregivers:* A Practical Guide for Getting Through the Day, Lowell House, Los Angeles, CA, 1996.

Hay, Louise L. *Gratitude: A Way of Life,* Hay House, Inc. Carlsbad, CA, 1996.

Ryan, M. J. *Attitudes of Gratitude:* How to Give and Receive Joy Every Day of Your Life, Conari Press, Berkeley, CA, 1999.

Vanzant, Iyanla, *Faith in the Valley:* Lessons for Women on the Journey to Peace. Fireside, New York, NY, 1996.

_____. *Acts of Faith:* Daily Meditations for People of Color. Fireside, New York, NY, 1993.

CHAPTER 3

Avadian, Brenda. *Where's My Shoes?* My Father's Walk Through Alzheimer's, North Star Books, Lancaster, CA, 1999.

Lanese, Janet. *Mothers are Like Miracles:* They Make Everything Possible, Fireside, New York, NY, 1998.

Loverde, Joy. *The Complete Eldercare Planner:* Where to Start, Questions to Ask, and How to Find Help, Silvercare Productions, New York, NY, 1997.

Pipher, Mary. *Another Country:* Navigating the Emotional Terrain of Our Elders, Riverhead Books, New York, NY, 1999.

Pitzele, Sefra Kobrin. *Kind Words for Caring People:* Daily Affirmations for Caregivers, Health Communications, Inc. Deerfield Beach, FL, 1993.

Thomas, William H. *Life Worth Living:* How Someone You Love Can Still Enjoy Life in a Nursing Home. The Eden Alternative in Action, VanderWyk & Burnham, Acton, MA, 1996.

Zgola, Jitka. *Care That Works:* A Relationship Approach to Persons with Dementia, The Johns Hopkins University Press, Baltimore, MD, 1999.

CHAPTER 4

Angel, Ronald J. and Angel, Jacqueline L. *Who Will Care for Us?* Aging and Long-term Care in Multicultural America, New York University Press, New York, NY, 1997.

Bell, Virginia and Troxel, David. *Best Friends Approach to Alzheimer's Care*, Health Professions Press, Baltimore, MD, 1997.

Bloomfield, Harold H. *Making Peace with Your Parents*: The Key to Enriching Your Life and All Your Relationships, Ballantine Books, New York, NY, 1983.

Forward, Susan. *Toxic Parents:* Overcoming Their Hurtful Legacy and Reclaiming Your Life, Bantam Books, New York, NY, 1989.

Larsen, Earnie and Hegarty, Carol Larsen. *Days of Healing, Days of Joy:* Daily Meditations for Adult Children, Hazelden Educational Materials, Center City, MN, 1987, 1992.

Lebow, Grace and Kane, Barbara. *Coping with Your Older Parent:* A Guide for Stressed-out Children, Avon Books, Inc., New York, NY, 1999.

Levin, Nora Jean. *How to Care for Your Parents*: A Practical Guide to Eldercare, W. W. Norton & Company, Inc., New York, NY, 1997.

Morris, Virginia. *How to Care for Aging Parents*, Workman Publishing Company, Inc., New York, NY, 1996.

CHAPTER 5

Astor, Bart. *Baby Boomer's Guide to Caring for Aging Parents*, A Spectrum Book, USA, 1998.

Benton, Christine M. Anthology: *A Mother's Book of Poems*, Contemporary Books, Inc. Chicago, IL, 1994.

Feil, Naomi. *The Validation Breakthrough*: Simple Techniques for Communicating with People with Alzheimer's-Type Dementia, Health Professions Press, Baltimore, MD, 1993.

Hodgson, Harriet. *Alzheimer's Finding the Words*: A Communication Guide for Those Who Care, CHRON IMED Publishing, Minneapolis, MN, 1995.

CHAPTER 6

Biziou, Barbara. *The Joy of Ritual*: Spiritual Recipes to Celebrate Milestones, Ease Transitions, and Make Every Day Sacred, Golden Book, New York, NY, 1999.

Brackey, Jolene. *Creating Moments of Joy*, Enhanced Living, Polk City, IA, 1999.

Dowling, James R. *Keeping Busy*: A Handbook of Activities for Persons with Dementia, The Johns Hopkins University Press, Baltimore, MD, 1995.

Mellon, Nancy. *The Art of Storytelling*, Element Books, Inc., Rockport, MA, 1992.

Osbeck, Kenneth W. *Amazing Grace:* 366 Inspiring Hymn Stories for Daily Devotions, Kregel Publications, Grand Rapids, MI, 1990.

Rosenbluth, Vera. *Keeping Family Stories Alive:* Discovering & Recording the Stories & Reflections of a Lifetime, Hartley & Marks Publishers, Inc. Point Roberts, WA, 1990.

Sheridan, Carmel. *Failure-Free Activities for the Alzheimer's Patient:* A Guidebook for Caregivers, Cottage Books, San Francisco, CA, 1987.

Walsh, Thomas F. *Favorite Hymns We learned in School,* Mercier Press, Niwot, CO, 1997.

Warren, Gwendolin Simms. *Ev'ry Time I Feel the Spirit:* 101 Best-loved Psalms, Gospel Hymns and Spiritual Songs of the African-American church, Henry Holt and Company, Inc. New York, NY, 1997.

CHAPTER 7

Fourteen Friends, LLC, *Fourteen Friends' Guide to Eldercaring:*
   Practical Advice, Inspiration, Shared Experiences, Space
   for Your Thoughts, Capital Books, Inc., Sterling, VA, 1999.

Unity School of Christianity. *Daily Word:* Silent Unity
   Magazine. Unity School of Christianity. Unity Village,
   MO, Vol. 136, No. 10, October, 1998.

## An Invitation

We invite you to share your visiting experience and contribute one
or more short stories for publication in our upcoming books about
visiting elders. We would appreciate short stories of up to 600 words
that have a positive, genuine direction. We are especially interested
in including stories from every ethnic, religious, racial, generation,
and international perspective. This way we will all learn more about
how the *world* visits. Your story and the author will receive credit
and our sincere thanks for each submission printed. Please send or
e-mail a copy of your story to:

ELDER Press, Inc.;
2370 Hwy. 89A;  Suite 11–#175;
Sedona, Arizona  86336
*sherry@eldervisit.org*

## About the Author

Sherry M. Bell, Ph.D. is the primary caregiver for her mother who has Alzheimer's Disease. She is also a writer intent on developing better ways to communicate with our elders. Sherry is a board member of the Arizona Chapter of the Alzheimer's Association and co-chair of Memory Walk-2000 for the Northern Arizona Region. She lives and writes in the beautiful, red-rock mountains of Sedona.